THE ANATOMY OF

HIGH PERFORMING TEAMS

A LEADER'S HANDBOOK

Marilyn Laiken

Guidance Series / 6

The Ontario Institute for Studies in Education / University of Toronto Press

An OISE / UT book published in association with UNIVERSITY OF TORONTO PRESS

Toronto Buffalo London

The Ontario Institute for Studies in Education of the University of Toronto is committed to the study of education and matters related to education in a social context in which learning is a life-long activity. OISE/UT was created in 1996. The result of the merger of the former OISE with the former Faculty of Education of the University of Toronto, it is one of the largest faculties of the University of Toronto and one of the largest faculties of education in North America.

University of Toronto Press Incorporated
Toronto Buffalo London

Canadian Cataloguing in Publication Data

Laiken, Marilyn E. (Marilyn, Edith), 1947–
    The anatomy of high performing teams : a leader's handbook

    ISBN 0-8020-8203-3

    1. Work groups. I. Title.

    HD66.L34 1998   658.4′02   C98-930511-2

    ISBN 0-8020-8203-3   Printed in Canada

CONTENTS

INTRODUCTION

Spinning Your Wheels

3

STORMING PHASE

The Group Takes Off

4

NORMING & PERFORMING PHASES

ACKNOWLEDGMENTS

How does one thank the many, many people whose ideas, energy and creativity over the years have contributed to this book?

To begin, I want to acknowledge the various group and team members I've had the privilege to work with during the past twenty years and whose patience often outlived my not always so helpful facilitation skills. They, along with Hedley Dimock, Dick McDonald, Matt Miles, Wil Schutz and Ken Blanchard taught me everything I know about working with people in groups.

The original draft of this book grew out of an Ontario Ministry of Tourism and Recreation project, initiated by Betsy Heatley and Lorraine Sutton, and carried on by Kathleen Howard, under the title of "Working With Community Groups". The leadership of these people and their editorial board was invaluable in initiating and contributing to the writing process.

The manuscript would still be on the shelf without the constant and continuing support of my colleagues and friends — in particular, David Kelleher, who said, "Why don't you publish this?"; Ron Smith, who consistently asks the key questions, and stimulates my creative thinking; Lanie Melamed, who along with her Concordia students read, critiqued and contributed their own ideas to the content; my O.D. support group colleagues, Diane Abbey-Livingston, Charlotte deHeinrich and Sandra Stark, and my dear friends Esther Kohn-Bentley and Timothy Bentley, who are always there for me, both personally and professionally.

Paul Lang, of ICON*MEDIA* (Desktop Publishing) maintained his delightful sense of humour through numerous drafts, and reminded me of the importance of having fun in the process.

For my family, and especially my life partner, Jeff Solway, who listened, read, critiqued, supported, offered insights and contributed the title, I realize that "thanks" is not enough.

Finally, I would like to express my appreciation to the Department of Adult Education at OISE, for providing the writing time which has allowed me to bring this project to completion, and to Hugh Oliver and Ann Nicholson at OISE Press for providing help in publishing it.

INTRODUCTION

In the high-performing organization – the organization of the twenty-first century – organizational goals and personal needs are met at one and the same time. The organizational culture is one of respect, responsibility and opportunity. Personal needs are met through the organization's achievements.

This vision of organization as a dynamic, creative environment, can only be a reality when it is driven by people-centred processes. Perhaps the most fundamental of these is the ability to work effectively in small groups. The functioning of work teams — their ability to set goals, establish priorities and resolve task-related problems, is critical to organizational effectiveness. Equally important, a high-performing work team unleashes the creative potential in each of its individual members.

> **Effective groups do not suddenly appear, fully developed and highly motivated. Like a garden, or an individual, work groups need careful and constant nurturing. Those entrusted with team leadership have a vital job to perform.**

Effective groups do not suddenly appear, fully developed and highly motivated. Like a garden, or an individual, work groups need careful and constant nurturing. Those entrusted with team leadership have a vital job to perform.

Leadership behaviour for team development stands in stark contrast to the traditional authority model. The truly effective group leader is enabling rather than controlling, empowering rather than overpowering, and facilitative rather than coercive.

Such leadership behaviours are not yet a familiar feature of our organizational landscapes. They are based on skills that many leaders and managers have yet to learn.

This manual provides a framework for building the skills and practices vital to the leadership of high performing teams. It is written in a manner which makes it useful to anyone wishing to learn more about the "art and science" of working with groups.

Managers at every level within organizations will find it helpful when they work collectively with their direct staff. Committee chairpersons and task force leaders will find it useful as they plan meetings which make the best possible use of time and resources. Similarly, the manual will be useful to community development workers and informal leaders in community groups. Finally, it should be particularly valuable to professional facilitators in their role as the leader's coach.

As an organizing framework, the manual uses a theory of group development (Tuckman, 1965) and a theory of leadership (Blanchard and Hersey, 1977). The interface of these theories is vital in understanding the group experience from the point of view of both the participant and the person who is providing leadership. A group which is developed with an understanding of these theories and how they interact is most likely to be capable of inspired performance.

> **Although grounded in theory, the manual's primary intention is to be of immediate use to practitioners.**

As theorist Kurt Lewin has said, "nothing is so practical as a good theory". Theory provides a dual framework: it helps explain choices and events reflectively, after the fact, and, used as a diagnostic tool, it will inform the practitioner's behaviour as s/he continues to work with groups.

Although grounded in theory, the manual's primary intention is to be of immediate use to practitioners. Thus, each section contains:

>**A** description of the phase of group development in which a group might be located, along with a guideline to help identify that phase

>**T**he problems and possibilities common to the phase, highlighting issues which should be considered in providing leadership to a group at this time

>**S**pecific leader and member behaviours which can help a group move through the phase, along with suggestions for exercises, activities, assessment forms, print and audio-visual resources.

The balance of this introduction summarizes the manual's conceptual framework for effective group leadership. Subsequent chapters will explore each component of the model in detail.

Facilitation
A Developmental Approach To Group Leadership

Traditionally, "LEADERSHIP" has been defined as a series of qualities or attributes which are found innately in some people and not in others. According to this view, only the select few have the capacity to be chairperson, group leader, supervisor, instructor or manager — while the others must be led, supervised, taught and managed.

FACILITATION on the other hand, may be defined as a series of learnable behaviours or roles which, when used skillfully with a group or individual, support others in:

Identifying clearly-defined, realistic and meaningful goals;

Establishing a plan of action for reaching these goals; and

Evaluating the outcome in terms of both the quality of the work accomplished, and satisfaction with the process by which the objectives are achieved.

The essential difference between the traditional concept of "leadership", and the concept of "facilitation" lies in whose goals are being met. This is an issue of power and authority — a question of who does what to whom, and why. The traditional leader is expected to perform all of the roles necessary to insure that the group functions smoothly. These include *task-related* activities such as organizing and defining roles and setting goals; or *relationship-related* activities such as ensuring effective communication among members, providing support, managing conflict and building productive work relationships.

The primary task is to help the group develop, from an initial dependence on the facilitator to provide the needed functions, to an eventual assumption of responsibility for sharing these roles among group members.

The effective facilitator views these activities, roles or functions as skill-related and learnable, rather than as attributable to his or her unique qualities as a leader.

The primary task is to help the group develop, from an initial dependence on the facilitator for providing the needed functions, to an eventual assumption of responsibility for sharing these roles among group members. It is not that the facilitator "gives up" responsibility — but that s/he focuses on helping others develop their ability to respond. The tasks continue to need doing, but instead of one person seeing him or herself as being in control of them, the control is shared by all members of the group.

This approach tends to greatly increase interest, motivation and accountability, and offers group members the opportunity to develop their own skills as facilitators and productive team contributors. At the same time, it provides the designated leader with eventual freedom from the responsibility of day-to-day group functioning. This allows the leader to focus on "boundary issues" such as helping to provide resources needed by the group (materials, information, etc.) and interfacing with the larger system of which the group may be part (government, community or the organization). It also permits the leader to move on to working with other, less developed groups, leaving those which are functioning effectively to do so essentially on their own.

> **This concept of "working oneself out of a job", either literally or figuratively, is the ultimate goal of the skillful facilitator.**

This concept of "working oneself out of a job", either literally or figuratively, is the ultimate goal of the skillful facilitator. However, it is not the point at which one generally begins in working with a group.

When group members meet initially to accomplish a task, they are usually not performing to their full potential. This may be due to a combination of factors: a lack of skill in providing the needed task and relationship functions; an automatic dependence on those in authority, which is fostered by our culture; and a lack of clarity regarding the expectations and goals of other members and the facilitator.

The Forming Phase

The initial stance in a new team tends to be one of dependence. members need to become oriented to the purpose of the group and the interests of individual members, and there is concern for safety and acceptance. People may be asking themselves such questions as "what are the 'rules' here?", and "will people like me and respect what I have to say?".

This stage in a group's development is referred to by Bruce Tuckman (1965) as the "forming" phase.

According to Ken Blanchard and Paul Hersey (1977), the appropriate behaviour for the facilitator at this stage is to structure and supervise activities carefully. The focus is on providing group members with an opportunity to meet each other, discuss personal needs related to the group's purpose, and become comfortable within the work setting.

The Storming Phase

Once group members feel included and "on board", they tend to begin taking more risks: they offer opinions, provide suggestions for both task and procedures, and generally attempt to influence the direction of decisions being made. At this stage, which is termed the "storming" phase in a group's development, there is often much tension and a sense of "spinning wheels", and of not accomplishing very much. Each member is vying for some control over the proceedings. This often involves a confrontation with the designated leader, who, at this point, has usually had the most influence in directing group activities.

The facilitative leader during the storming phase will help group members acknowledge their frustrations and anger, help surface and manage conflicts which arise, and generally resist trying to solve problems or encourage the group to reach agreements at this point.

The process is similar to a teenager's "separation" from significant adults in order to begin asserting his or her own independence. The climate in the group at this time tends to be stormy, with people complaining vehemently about the lack of progress, but offering much resistance to anyone who attempts to help move the group along.

The facilitative leader during the storming phase will help group members acknowledge their frustrations and anger, surface and manage conflicts which arise, and generally resist trying to solve problems or encourage the group to reach agreements at this point.

Eventually, members will make a suggestion which counters one of the leader's original proposals or organizing structures for the group. If the leader goes along with the suggestion, rather than arguing against it, the group may move through its storming phase. People will begin to establish norms based on the wishes of all group members, including, but not only, those of the group leader.

If, however, the group's attempt at independence at this stage is blocked by a facilitator who fears "losing control", or becomes panicked by the conflictual atmosphere, it will likely regress to a dependent stage from which it may never again resurface.

The Norming And Performing Phases

If the group successfully moves through its storming phase, with a leader who has mainly stayed out of the way, it will enter a cathartic period of relief, called the "honeymoon" or "norming" phase. Members will congratulate themselves and each other on being a "great group". However, like all honeymoons, this is a brief respite, for group members quickly recognize the need to move on with their task.

This final stage of development, termed the "performing" phase is usually the most productive in terms of task accomplishment. It is a time in which the group members function in a truly interdependent manner. They share the leadership roles, set realistic goals, communicate openly and provide honest feedback to each other, handle conflict constructively, recognize and use one another's strengths, solve problems and make decisions in a way which takes all members' opinions into account.

The facilitator, on the other hand, gains power by empowering others to meet their individual and collective goals. Of this leader, as Lao Tzu points out, "... in the end, they will all say, *we did it ourselves*".

It is this phase which was described earlier as the ultimate goal of the effective facilitator. The leader's role at this point is to function more as an ordinary group member, than as one with a significantly different status. Of course, his or her status in reality remains different, to the extent s/he may move on to working with another group, or spend time performing the role of "boundary buffer" previously described.

It is also important to note that although the group as a whole may be proceeding through the phases at one rate of development, various individuals may be proceeding through them at different rates.

An important role of the facilitator is to be sensitive to such individual differences, and to work with these members — perhaps between sessions. Sometimes a five or ten-minute update before the meeting for a member who has missed a session will help him or her feel included. A chance to openly express some concern may help a member move through his or her own "storming" phase, and become a more productive contributor to the group.

In addition, the group will cycle through the phases a number of times during its "lifetime", usually moving through them in reverse order as it ends its work as a unit. However, the length of time required for each phase will become progressively shorter, and the movement through the phases will be less and less noticeable.

The major implication for the facilitator of accepting this developmental approach to group leadership is the need to redefine the meaning of having "power", and feeling "in control".

The more traditional view of power implies control *over* others, or the ability to direct their actions to a specific end — one usually designated by the leader. The facilitator, on the other hand, gains power by *empowering others* to meet their individual and collective goals. Of this leader, as the ancient Chinese philosopher Lao Tzu wrote many centuries ago, "... in the end, they will all say, *we did it ourselves*". ❖

GROUP DEVELOPMENT and FACILITATIVE LEADERSHIP

Phases of Group Development
(needs of group members)

Role of the Facilitator

Over time...

Terminating the group's work

ADJOURNING

▷ Creates apprehension, minor crisis

▷ Regression in maturity level

▷ Needing help in saying "good-bye"

DELEGATING / SEPARATING

▷ Supporting, letting go

▷ Adjusting own leadership style

▷ Helping group deal with termination issues

Functioning as an effective group

PERFORMING

▷ Working productively toward shared goals

▷ Problem solving and decision-making

▷ Open communication, trust, respect

▷ Dealing with conflict

SUPPORTING

▷ Offering own resources, ideas

▷ Sharing the leadership role

Managing conflict, establishing "ground rules"

NORMING

▷ Resolving control concerns

▷ Establishing group agreement

▷ Catharsis, "honeymoon"

▷ Being available for one-to-one consultation/coaching

▷ Smoothing the interface between the group & the organization or community

Dealing with issues of power and control

STORMING

▷ Consolidating influence

▷ Confronting dependency on leader

▷ Conflict among group members

▷ Work level low

COACHING

▷ Surfacing issues, legitimizing concerns

▷ Facilitating communication, managing conflict

▷ Inviting input and feedback, sharing control

▷ Expecting and accepting tension

Developing a positive working environment

FORMING

▷ Becoming oriented

▷ Developing commitment

▷ Needing direction

▷ Wanting to be accepted, included

DIRECTING

▷ Climate setting

▷ Clarifying roles, expectations

▷ Defining goals, providing structure

▷ Group building

CREDITS: Model by Marilyn Laiken (1985); graphic design, Jeff Solway (1988); "phases of group development" headings, Bruce Tuckman (1965); "role of the facilitator" headings, K. Blanchard (1985)

REFLECTION

Create a personal case study

In order to begin applying the material which follows directly to your own situation, think about a group with which you are presently working or with which you plan to be working. . .

- Identify the group.

  Payroll Team

- Why does this group meet?

  ?

- What is the group's history (how long has it been meeting; how much turnover has it experienced in membership, leadership)?

  Teleworkers → to be returned to business work location.

- What expectations do group members have of you in your role? What are your own expectations of yourself?

  Understand what truly they do. Provide coaching & feedback, development is my focus

You may find it useful to keep your "case" in mind as we begin to explore the life of a group in Chapter 1. ❖

1

PRE-MEETING PREPARATION

HAVE YOU EVER:

. . . gone to a meeting that started late, or had already begun, when you thought you were on time?

. . . arrived at the wrong place, or on the wrong day?

. . . sat through the first session of a meeting, and then realized you shouldn't even be there?

You, as a group leader, can help your members avoid such frustrating experiences by doing some careful planning before your group meets for the first time.

The following section will help you learn about:

      How to decide on who should attend your group meetings;

      How to assess group members' needs and interests;

      How to welcome participants and prepare them;

      How to ensure a comfortable physical environment.

Since we are assuming that the group has not yet formed at this point, the information in this chapter precedes the use of group development theory. However it provides the foundation upon which a group can develop successfully. Solid work " *behind the scenes*" on your part insures that the group will at least be starting with all of the necessary building blocks in place!

First Contacts

Any contact which you make with participants prior to the first meeting of your group will begin to set the "climate" in which members can expect to work. This may be a telephone call to schedule the meeting date and time; a questionnaire distributed as a preliminary needs assessment; or a mailed agenda establishing the focus for the first session.

In each case, the recipient will begin to form an impression of you, their facilitator, as representative of the kind of experience they can expect in your group. It is in this preliminary contact that you can begin to establish norms for treating people with respect — offering them options and demonstrating flexibility; providing them with a sense that their opinions and preferences are important, and will be attended to; and by providing information, helping to alleviate some of the anxiety that the first meeting of a new group inevitably engenders.

Who Should Attend?

If the membership of your group has not yet been determined, it may become your responsibility to propose or decide on whom to invite.

Of course, this decision should be based primarily on the reasons why the group is meeting, and who would be most likely to make a substantial contribution to that purpose.

However, the "stakeholder" concept is also important here. In addition to asking yourself "who can contribute to what we're doing?", you might also ask yourself "who is likely to impede the progress of this group if they are not included?". Anyone who will be directly affected by, or has a "stake" in the decisions which the group will make, should either be included, consulted or kept informed on a regular basis. This decision is ultimately best made by the group itself, once you have a core membership — however, it may also influence who is invited to attend the first session.

You might begin the first meeting of an on-going group by asking the members to look around and tell you whether there is anyone missing who they think should be there. You can then discuss the reasons for their suggestions, and together decide whether or not to extend an invitation.

In a continuing group, there may be a need to periodically reassess the membership in terms of:

Potential contribution of each member, given possibly redefined purposes;

Continuing interest in participating;

Stakeholder investment;

The number of group members (which probably should not exceed 8-10 for an on-going group).

You may find that some members are looking for a relatively "painless" excuse to exit, or that others who had not been considered should be included.

And now, the sticky question — what if you have members who are no longer making a contribution, but who do not wish to leave?

You will probably first want to provide feedback to the group member(s) in question privately, and discuss the situation with them.

You may need to collect more information on why someone who originally made a contribution is no longer able to do so. Perhaps the goals of the group have changed, and are no longer meeting the needs of some members. However, these members remain because they are attracted by the social aspects of belonging to the group.

In this case, you might consider creating sub-groups with specific tasks to accomplish which are more responsive to these members needs, and also contribute to some aspect of the group's purpose. The sub-group members might report to the total group periodically, but do not necessarily need to attend every meeting. It is likely that such a solution would both provide relief for the disinterested members, and alleviate frustration for the remainder of the group.

If there is a need to actually help people exit from the group permanently, there should be some objective basis for making such a decision (especially if the member in question is reluctant to comply). Member "job descriptions", or a revised mandate for the group which specifies tasks for individual members can be useful here.

However, be cautious in making such interventions, and be certain that your diagnosis is based on the expressed goals of the group, and not on personal (and sometimes hidden) agendas.

Needs Assessment
The "Bottom Line" Of Group Facilitation

Once you have determined who the group members will be, you will want to spend some time assessing their needs and interests in relation to the purpose(s) of the group. This information will eventually provide the basis for setting mutually agreed-upon goals — the first step in effective group facilitation.

The process of gathering this information is commonly referred to as "needs assessment". The results obtained through this procedure are not a set of goals, but simply a collection of preferences and interests of individual members. Once these are made known to the group, there still remains the task of finding common areas and negotiating differences in order to finally reach agreement on group goals in which all members are willing to invest their energies.

There are a variety of purposes for conducting a needs assessment:

If the intention is to design a skill training session, the facilitator will probably have some personal investment in what is to presented or learned. In this case, a needs assessment prior to the event might serve a dual purpose: checking on the appropriateness of the intended content focus, and helping plan for the session in a way that ensures meeting participants' needs. By allowing participants input through the needs assessment, the facilitator enhances their commitment to the eventual design.

A needs assessment in a new group, as mentioned previously, can provide the basis for setting task directions for the group.

A needs assessment may be used in an on-going group to periodically reformulate task goals and to check on members' satisfaction with the way the group is functioning.

For a group which is representing the needs of others (ie: a community group), a needs assessment can be designed by the group for use within the community to help group members respond more fully to their constituents' concerns.

Needs assessment techniques

A needs assessment may be as simple or as intricate as the resources available permit or the situation demands. The technology may involve complicated scientific survey design, or may be as basic as asking people to describe, in their own words, what their interests are within a specified area. The bottom line is to collect the data which is most relevant to helping you and the group establish priorities for action.

You will probably find most useful the results collected from relatively simple, open-ended questions which yield a narrative rather than a numerical response.

These questions can be asked in one of at least three ways:

1. Verbally, prior to the meeting, either through a telephone or face-to-face interview;

2. In written form, through a questionnaire prior to the meeting;

3. "On-the-spot", at the beginning of, or during the meeting. Each of these methods is described in detail below.

Verbal Needs Assessment
(by telephone or in person)

If time and resources make it feasible, a personal interview, as opposed to one by telephone, is preferable. In person, people tend to relax and chat more informally, and are likely to mention areas by chance which would not be raised in more formal telephone contact.

Several guidelines for this type of data collection are:

Spend time in establishing meaningful contact with the interviewee. Explain the purpose of the interview, and describe how you will use the data. Stress confidentiality, if this is an important factor.

Take hand-written notes while the interview proceeds. If this is difficult, a tape recorder can be useful — but it may cause the interviewee some discomfort, and could result in more censored information. In addition, it will multiply your time or financial expenditure, as tapes will need to be transcribed.

Particularly for the inexperienced interviewer, it will be helpful to have prepared a structured list of questions, which can act as a guideline for your conversation.

Of the data collection techniques, the personal interview tends to be the most informative, but also the most time-consuming. It is particularly useful when the number of participants is small (ten to twelve). With larger numbers, you might consider interviewing a representative cross-section of the participants, or conducting small group instead of individual interviews. (These are commonly referred to as "focus groups".)

In using "representatives", be aware that representatives are rarely that. Unless they've done a poll of their constituency, they are likely to be speaking mostly for themselves. Use their responses with that possibility in mind.

Focus groups may provide less candid responses than would individual interviews — although members of a focus group can often spark each other's ideas in ways which provide for richer data.

Telephone interviews are more subject to interruption than personal ones, and tend to feel more formal. However, they may be less time consuming — especially if you make an appointment with respondents, so that they are prepared for the interview and have cleared a time during which they will not be interrupted. This also demonstrates some respect for the fact that they may not be able to drop everything (especially during a working day) in order to engage in an on-the-spot question and answer session.

The Written Questionnaire

This is a more expedient form of needs assessment than any previously described. It can also be highly informative, if the questionnaire is properly constructed.

Although there are some "do's" and "don'ts", one does not require a course in test construction to design a useful needs assessment tool. You simply need to decide on what you want to know for your purposes — and then design questions which clearly and directly ask for the information.

Try to avoid questions which elicit a "yes" or "no" response, as they offer little real information. The intention is not so much to easily tabulate results and produce a numerical picture, but rather, to allow people to express their needs and preferences openly, using their own words.

Finally, it is often useful to consult with potential or past participants in constructing the questionnaire. No one knows better than those who will be asked to answer the questions which ones are likely to spark their imagination!

Following is a sample needs assessment form which you might use to help you construct your own questionnaire.

Needs Assessment Questionnaire

In order to help with my planning for our first meeting, as well as to help gear your thinking to our project, I would appreciate your thoughtful responses to the following questions.

A collated summary of these will be presented during our first session together, in order to help us begin to set our goals as a group.

1. What information (if any) have you received about the purposes of this group?

. . . .

2. Of the purposes mentioned, in which areas are you most interested?

. . . .

3. Are there other areas in which you would like to have our group work?

. . . .

4. What do you particularly hope to gain for yourself from being a member of this group?

. . . .

5. What are the particular skills or experiences which you can offer this group in its tasks?

. . . .

6. Do you have any concerns about being a member of this group?

. . . .

7. Do you have specific preferences for times and meeting places for our group?

. . . .

8. Any other comments or suggestions you would like to make at this time?

. . . .

Thanks for your help !

Other examples of questionnaires and further details on their construction may be found in Diane Abbey-Livingston's and David Abbey's publication entitled "Enjoying Research? A How To Manual on Needs Assessment" (1982)

On-The-Spot Data Collection

The final method proposed here is probably the simplest, and often the most effective, because of its immediacy. It requires no preliminary time or effort, and serves to both orient the group to the task at hand, and inform the facilitator of individual and group priorities. This type of needs assessment may take any number of forms. Some ideas which you might find useful are:

Going around the group to provide each member with the opportunity to state his or her "hopes" and "concerns" regarding the project. This can also be done in sub-groups, with each group reporting back a summary of its members' responses. The role of the facilitator is to record (word-for-word) what each group or member reports, on a flip chart pad. These responses can then be posted in the meeting room for future reference.

Presenting a "menu" of possible goal areas, with members asked to rank them in order of interest. A variation is a group "brainstorm" to generate the areas, which are then evaluated by mutual preference.

As mentioned previously, the group's goals may be dictated by the community which it is designed to serve. In this case, it may be wise to propose the option of sub-grouping to create "ad hoc" committees, with members focusing most of their energies on the areas of greatest interest to them. The key point is that people will devote their best efforts to those tasks in which they are personally most invested.

REFLECTION - Do you have other ideas for how to conduct an on-the-spot data collection with a group?

Several potential pitfalls in all of the methods which have been outlined are:

If people have been given information about the group prior to the first meeting, they will tend to feed back to you what they have heard.

It is often not until well into the process of meeting regularly that individuals or the group as a whole will have a clear sense of real goals to which people can feel committed.

Group goals are difficult to formulate during the initial stages of group development, when the focus is primarily on meeting individual needs, and reducing the anxiety produced by an unfamiliar situation.

All of this underlines the importance of ensuring that the assessment of needs and the setting of group goals becomes an integral part of the group's work together. Both needs and goals change over time, and issues which once seemed pressing may be obsolete or insignificant later in the life of an on-going group.

Collating, interpreting and using the information

An interview or narrative questionnaire will produce vast amounts of information which, unlike that from a quantitatively-designed instrument, will require much time and energy to summarize.

Nevertheless, the quantity and quality of information which these methods yield is far more useful for the purpose of setting objectives than would be a set of numerical responses. The time expenditure is well worth the effort in the long run.

An approach which works well is to summarize the responses for one question at a time — retaining the original words where possible. You can then note with a check-mark beside the statement each time the same sentiment or idea is repeated.

It is important not to do any interpreting or editing of responses at this point, but simply to report at face value what has been said. If you provide an interpretation, respondents are less likely to trust that the data truly reflects their ideas.

Once the information has been collated and summarized, it is crucial that it be fed back to the respondents in some form. You may choose to summarize the results in writing and distribute a copy to each participant before you meet. However, you might find it more effective to present the data to the group on flip charts during your first meeting, and then hand out the written summary. In this way, you or other group members can respond immediately to questions of clarification, omissions and misrepresentations.

This type of activity provides a useful method for beginning a group meeting. It is logical to follow such a presentation with a discussion about directions and format, and leads naturally into encouraging members to begin to take responsibility for organizing the tasks of the group.

Summary
Key Points About Using Needs Assessments

Common Varieties Of Needs Assessment Include:

Input from workshop participants on the content and format for the program;

Input from members of a new group, to begin goal-setting;

Input from members of an on-going group to continually reassess and reformulate their goals;

Input from community members to provide direction for a decision-making group which represents them.

Techniques:

Verbal assessment through telephone or face-to-face interviews

Written questionnaires

On-the-spot data collection such as:

- going around the group (or sub-group);
- choices for goals/projects made from a "menu" constructed by the group, or presented by the facilitator;
- community focus groups.

"Ground Rules" For Using The Information:

Always present back to your respondents a summarized version of the data which you have collected.

Try as much as possible to summarize data without interpretation.

A narrative, or open-ended format will provide the most useful information, but be certain that the questions cannot be answered with a yes/no response.

Provide participants with an opportunity to respond to the collated data, so that they can share in the responsibility for acting on the results.

Planning For The First Meeting

Defining Preliminary Objectives, and Orienting Group Members Prior to the First Meeting

The results of the needs assessment will offer you the basis for planning your first meeting. A briefly summarized version of the results (which can be expanded upon during the meeting), along with an outline of a proposed agenda, will provide the basis for a welcome "letter" which can serve as an orientation for group members prior to the session.

You may also choose to include preparatory reading materials which will help participants focus on the content of the meeting.

However, keep in mind that unless you have given specific instructions that the material be read, some members will have done so, while others will not. Therefore, either allow some time during the meeting to review the material, or do not design it in as a specific content focus (it might just be considered "background reading"). Otherwise, you will have set up a competitive environment in which some members will feel "one-down" before they utter their first comments!

A "welcome letter" is a useful way to help participants feel expected, and somewhat prepared for their first encounter with their new group.

Some tips on how to write a welcome letter:

Remember that this is one of your first contacts with group members, and will help to form their expectations about the experience.

Keep your summary of the needs assessment results simple — a few key points which seem to be thematic, and which have influenced directly the focus for the first meeting will serve the purpose.

A "proposed" agenda is precisely that — participants may want to influence it as you begin the meeting, so you will want to allow some flexibility for unplanned-for items. Therefore, outline items briefly, but don't assign exact times to each in the preliminary agenda. However, if the meeting is more than a couple of hours, you may want to note break and meal times, as well as starting and ending times — and then be prepared to stick to them, unless they are renegotiated by the group.

If the session is to take place in a residential setting (participants "live in" for a few days in a retreat environment), be sure to include information about the facility so that participants will know what to bring in the way of recreational equipment, clothing, etc. It will be helpful to emphasize the informality of dress, if that is the intention, and to encourage people to bring along musical instruments or games for group entertainment — especially if the environment is "rustic".

Even if the environment is residential, people may be tempted to squeeze in a meeting or a visit home. Consider discouraging that in the welcome letter, emphasizing the need for consistency in membership to make the most of an intensive group experience. Obviously, there may be some instances which are unavoidable, but a word from you on that topic may help to minimize unnecessary disruption to the group.

Ensuring a comfortable physical "climate" for your meeting:

Location planning

John Ingalls, in "*A Trainer's Guide to Andragogy*" (1973), notes that the key elements to "climate-setting" in the physical area are:

- comfort
- variety
- mobility
- sensory accommodation.

Obviously, you will be limited by the physical surroundings available in considering each of these factors. However, you can use your own creative resources, and those of your group members, to make a less than perfect environment more comfortable.

Key areas to consider in planning the physical environment are:

Adequate lighting — preferably natural light from windows; but if this is not available, lamps help "warm up" fluorescent lighting;

Reasonable acoustics and noise control — minimize disruption;

Adequate ventilation, and if possible, thermostatically controlled room temperature, which you can adjust;

Comfortable furnishings which can be easily moved, to allow for a variety of formats in your seating arrangements. A useful format is a circular or square table for easy discussion, with room at the perimeter to allow for sub-grouping, if necessary. Obviously, the room set-up will vary with the purpose and design of the meeting, and should be adjusted to meet those needs. For instance, a discussion would require a round-table format; whereas viewing a film or hearing a presentation would be more comfortable in a theatre-style format;

Clear directions to help people reach the facility, and adequate parking space once they arrive;

Signs in the building to help a new group find the meeting location;

If possible, a ready supply of coffee, tea and juice to help people enter informally — particularly during the first session;

Any audio-visual equipment which may be required, such as flip-chart easels, pads and markers, film, slide or overhead projectors, a screen, pens and paper.

A note on the use of flip-charts:

In on-going meetings, the use of a flip chart to help all members focus on the same item is more effective than having one member keep notes which no one else will see until they receive them in the form of minutes some time later. Notes taken on a flip chart (by the facilitator, or a meeting "recorder") can be either typed up verbatim, or used as a basis for writing up the meeting minutes. Apart from helping the group to focus, flip-charts have the added advantage of allowing members to correct misinterpretations as they occur, rather than through the minutes at the following meeting. They can also be displayed on the wall during the meeting to help group members share the responsibility of keeping the group on track.

Are there other creative ways in which you have used flip-charts, or have seen them or other audio-visual equipment used in meetings?. . .

Preparing equipment and resource materials

It is difficult to over-emphasize the importance of being fully prepared! Murphy's Law of Meetings states that "if anything can go wrong, it will". However, careful pre-meeting preparation can help you outsmart Murphy, or at least forestall some of the more obvious potential problems. Working with groups is a complex enough task, without further complicating it by not having an extra bulb or extension cord for the overhead projector, or by finding that the room you've booked to comfortably accommodate twelve people, actually seats five with a squeeze!

For these reasons, you will want to plan to arrive at the meeting location early enough to make last minute changes, if necessary, and to give yourself a chance to relax and focus before the session begins. "Early birds" who appear fifteen minutes before the scheduled starting time are often willing to give a hand with the room set-up, and this can help break the ice for them.

Reading materials/handouts

Back-up reading materials, particularly for a training session, are usually very much appreciated by participants. Some tips in preparing these are:

- The content should be directly related to the material which is to be covered in the sessions.

- One good article/handout is more useful than three mediocre ones.

- Page numbers and coloured tabs or differently coloured divider sheets help with easy access to materials which will be referred to during the session.

- If overhead slides are used, people seem to appreciate having a copy of these included in their handout package, so that they can participate fully in the discussion, rather than having to take notes. However people often want to take notes as well, so include some blank paper or have some lined pads on hand (even responsible adults sometimes forget to bring such equipment to meetings!).

- Reading materials which are expected to be discussed during the session should be sent out well in advance of the meeting, with some indication about how they will be used.

Following is a check-list to help you prepare for the organizational aspects of your meetings.

MEETING PREPARATION FORM

Name of Group _____

Meeting Number _____ Date _____

Purpose of Meeting: (Briefly)

_____

Who is expected to attend:

_____

Physical set-up of meeting room:

_____

Equipment Checklist:

- ☐ flip chart easels, pads, pens
- ☐ slide projector and screen
- ☐ overhead projector and screen
- ☐ film projector, screen and film
- ☐ tape recorder
- ☐ vcr and monitor
- ☐ spare bulbs and extension cords
- ☐ name cards and tags (for a new group)
- ☐ workbooks, folders, handout materials
- ☐ spare pens and paper
- ☐ other...

Refreshments for "Nutrition Breaks" _____

_____

Pre-meeting Preparation Materials

(What, to whom, when to be sent) _____

_____

Other: _____

_____

So — you've done your homework! You've assessed needs and prepared group members for what to expect in your first meeting. You've checked on the meeting room, and decided on the set-up, and you've ordered all audio-visual equipment and materials you might need. You've even managed to ensure that refreshments will be awaiting the arrival of your group.

The next question, then, as the popular book puts it, is, "What do you say after you say hello?"

The following chapter will focus on establishing effective "*beginnings*" in a new group, and help you answer such questions as:

How do I help group members (and myself) handle the first tense moments in a new group?

How do I help people get acquainted, and begin to establish productive group norms?

How do I help clarify what members can expect of me as their group "facilitator"?

How do we use the needs assessment results to start setting group goals, and developing commitment to the task at hand?

2

BACKGROUND

General Principles of Group Development

AS WE NOTED IN THE INTRODUCTION, this manual's organizing framework is a combination of group development and leadership theory. Before we begin describing the phases, and the leadership behaviours which are most facilitative in each, it may be useful to understand some of the basic principles underlying the concept of "group development".

Research (see "print resources" at the end of this section for references) has demonstrated that groups experience predictable phases of development, much the same as individuals do in their growth, whether they are together for three days, one week, one month, or several years.

These phases cannot be skipped or initiated externally. However, they can be facilitated by the use of specific leadership skills, so that the group does not become arrested in one phase.

It is not until a group has moved through all phases of development at least once that it is able to begin performing at an optimal level.

The phases will be repeated over and over, at ever-increasing depth, and the group will move from one phase to the next more and more quickly.

Individual members may be experiencing the phases at different rates from each other, and from that of the group as a whole.

Why focus on understanding group development theory?

As a group leader, you will be much more able to respond appropriately to the specific needs of the group, and plan for ways to help it develop through each phase. An understanding of group development theory will allow you to work with the inevitable development of the group, rather than against it.

It will help you feel less personally defensive, as the group challenges your leadership during its "storming" phase.

It will allow you to help members understand and learn from their own developmental experience as a group.

The following sections of the manual will enable you to:

Identify each of the developmental phases, as your group is experiencing it;

Examine in detail the specific issues which each phase raises;

Determine some helpful facilitator interventions which will enable the group to move through the phase in which it is located.

REFLECTION - Reflect back on how you felt and what you thought as you entered some first-time gathering. List your thoughts here. . .

It is likely that you have just outlined the important aspects of the first phase of group development — the "forming" phase. The following section will describe that phase in more detail.

GROUP DEVELOPMENT AND FACILITATIVE LEADERSHIP

Phases of Group Development (needs of group members)

Role of the Facilitator

Over time...

Terminating the group's work

ADJOURNING
▷ Creates apprehension, minor crisis
▷ Regression in maturity level
▷ Needing help in saying "good-bye"

DELEGATING/SEPARATING
▷ Supporting, letting go
▷ Adjusting own leadership style
▷ Helping group deal with termination issues

Functioning as an effective group

PERFORMING
▷ Working productively toward shared goals
▷ Problem solving and decision-making
▷ Open communication, trust, respect
  Dealing with conflict

SUPPORTING
▷ Offering own resources, ideas
▷ Sharing the leadership role

Managing conflict, establishing "ground rules"

NORMING
▷ Resolving control concerns
▷ Establishing group agreement
▷ Catharsis, "honeymoon"

▷ Being available for one-to-one consultation/coaching
▷ Smoothing the interface between the group & the organization or community

---

Dealing with issues of power and control

STORMING
▷ Consolidating influence
▷ Confronting dependency on leader
▷ Conflict among group members
▷ Work level low

COACHING
▷ Surfacing issues, legitimizing concerns
▷ Facilitating communication, managing conflict
▷ Inviting input and feedback, sharing control
▷ Expecting and accepting tension

Developing a positive working environment

FORMING
▷ Becoming oriented
▷ Developing commitment
▷ Needing direction
▷ Wanting to be accepted, included

DIRECTING
▷ Climate setting
▷ Clarifying roles, expectations
▷ Defining goals, providing structure
▷ Group building

CREDITS: Model by Marilyn Laiken (1985); graphic design, Jeff Solway (1988); "phases of group development" headings, Bruce Tuckman (1965); "role of the facilitator" headings, K. Blanchard (1985)

FORMING PHASE

How Do I Recognize It?

This initial phase of group development is usually experienced by a new group, or an on-going group confronted with a new structure or task, or a change in membership.

In the forming phase, group members may lack skill or experience in doing the task at hand, and are also probably lacking in their ability to function effectively as a group. They may be unclear about their expectations of each other, and the group leader's expectations of them; and are probably unsure about the roles each of them will play in the work of the group.

As a result, group members will exhibit more dependency on the designated leader of the group than at any other time in the group's development. This is indicated by relatively passive behaviour — waiting to be told what to do and how to do it; looking at the leader rather than at each other when making comments in the group; a lack of confrontation with the leader or each other. At the same time, the leader and fellow members are being "sized up." Communication will be contained and polite ("coffee-talk"), and the work level will be relatively low, as the concerns of group members are individually-oriented.

What Do Group Members Need?

The need of group members at this time is to become oriented to the group's purposes, its ground rules for functioning together, and the roles that various members, including the leader, will play.

They will be concerned with their "hygiene needs" (ie: physical comfort in the work setting) and personal acceptance needs (ie: "how will I be treated here; will I be accepted and acknowledged?"). Members will also be examining their own commitment to the group and its purposes ("what's in it for me to participate here?").

The major need is to begin developing open communication and interaction with other group members, in order to build a sense of trust. This eventually allows members to freely offer their unique skills and resources to the group.

A useful summary (author unknown) is provided here as a "handout" which you might want to use in helping your group begin to share the responsibility of meeting individual needs, as well as group goals.

Basic Needs Of People In Groups

In order for me to be comfortable, interested and productive in a group, the leader or the other group members must take into account the fact that. . .

1. I need a sense of belonging. (I want to be wanted).
    - a feeling that no one objects to my presence
    - a feeling that I am sincerely welcome
    - a feeling that I am honestly needed for my total self, not just for my hands, my money, etc.

2. I need to have a share in planning the group goals. (My need will be satisfied only when I feel that my ideas have had a fair hearing).

3. I need to feel that the goals are within reach and that they make sense to me.

4. I need to feel that what I'm doing has real purpose, and contributes to the life of the group — that its values may extend even beyond the group itself.

5. I need to share in making the rules of the group — the rules which determine how we interact and work toward our goals.

6. I need to know just what is expected of me so that I can work confidently.

7. I need to have responsibilities that challenge, that are within range of my abilities and interests, and that contribute towards reaching our goals.

8. I need to see that progress is being made toward the goals we have set.

9. I need to be kept informed. What I'm not up on, I may be down on.

10. I need to have confidence in our leader or group — confidence based on trust, openness and feedback within the group.

In brief, regardless of how much sense it makes to the leader or the group, the situation in which I find myself must make sense to me.

People gain their initial inclusion into groups in various ways. Some are very quiet, observing carefully those around them. Others don't feel included until they have been heard, by expressing opinions, telling jokes or asking questions. Still others make their initial contacts one-on-one, and then feel freer to speak in front of the group as a whole.

- What is your "inclusion pattern" as you enter a new group? Does it change, depending on the nature of the group or its purpose?

- As a group leader, what have you done, or would you do, to help others gain their inclusion in a new group?

What Can The Facilitator Do?

Following are some further suggestions to add to your list. They are categorized into three main areas:

- Establishing a comfortable emotional environment;

- Clarifying expectations, setting group goals and developing commitment;

- Defining your role as group facilitator.

Generally, helpful facilitator behaviour in this phase involves structuring and directing activities closely; helping people to become comfortable in the work setting; and providing designed opportunities for group-building, sharing expectations, and setting some preliminary group goals.

The following section will provide you with specific ideas about how facilitate a group effectively through the "forming" phase in its development.

Establishing A Comfortable Psychological / Emotional Working Environment

The task of developing a positive environment is ultimately shared by the facilitator and the group members. However, as in all other aspects of the group's development, the initial responsibility lies with the designated leader of the group. The manner in which this task is handled will have a direct influence on everything else which occurs in the members' experience. It is the foundation upon which a solid, effective working group is built, and no amount of skill in other aspects of facilitation can replace a deficiency of attention to this area.

Greeting the participants

Most people bring to meetings with other adults some degree of anxiety and uncertainty, and will appreciate you helping them "aboard". Participants should be greeted at the door and welcomed into the room. A name tag will allow them and you begin to address each other personally, and may also be used as an ice-breaker, if it includes a word about interests, special skills, etc. Note, however, that it is important here to keep the level of risk as low as possible. You might request first names only, in large letters written with dark marker, so that the name can be read across a table. Allowing people to make up their own name tags permits them to use nick-names of which you might not be aware. Also, having empty tags avoids forcing people to sit in the seat which you have designated by a prepared name tag or place marker.

It is wise to design into the schedule a "flow-in" period of ten to fifteen minutes, to allow for informal chit-chat over coffee. Since you can assume that some people will inevitably be late for the first session, this also avoids having to begin with several participants missing, or adding time pressure in order to cover the agenda. In following meetings or sessions, you might then propose a norm of starting and ending on time with whomever is present — although the group might decide formally that "starting on time" includes a ten minute flow-in period. The final conclusion to this and any other discussion regarding group "norms" (such as smoking guidelines) is less important than the fact that discussion on the issue is initiated and explicitly decided by the group, or, in the early stages of development, proposed by the leader.

Getting acquainted – "ice-breakers"

Once participants are settled and ready to begin work, a fifteen-minute to one-half hour activity can help them get acquainted, presuming they are strangers to one another. Particularly for a group which will be meeting regularly over a period of weeks or months, a few minutes early in the first session will have a significant impact on helping to develop the cohesiveness necessary for effective functioning. Additionally, it helps you and the group over the first awkward moments by enlisting the active participation of every member. Even for those who tend to be quiet in a group, this will help "break the ice" and they should find it easier to speak up in future sessions.

Following are several methods which you may find useful.

For a LARGE GROUP (more than 12-15), SUB-GROUPS may be created to do one of the following:

Develop a creative way to present to the total group a summary of the interests and resources of group members.

Individuals introduce themselves to the sub-group on the basis of their particular interest in the topic at hand; then the sub-group summarizes these statements (on a flip-chart or verbally) to the total group.

Individuals list on a flip chart what they can "give" to and what they hope to "get" from this group. These are then posted so that members can read them and begin to discuss with each other their particular interests and skills.

For a SMALLER GROUP (less than 15):

Individuals pair and introduce themselves to their partner, or are "interviewed" by their partner i or approximately five minutes each. Each partner then introduces the other to the rest of the group. NOTE: *It is fair to warn the partners that they will be asked to do this introduction while the activity is being assigned — no surprises, please!*

Round Robin — each person around the table is asked to say something about him or herself. The facilitator might structure this more by offering a specific focus (ie: "your most unusual trait"). Alternately, the group can be asked to brainstorm a list of things they would like to know about each other, and each person chooses one to respond to during his or her turn.

Cold Introductions — for a group in which members know each other, but to whom the facilitator is new. Each person around the table asks another from anywhere in the room to introduce him or her briefly to the group. People tend to be interested, and often flattered, to hear what others would choose to say about them spontaneously!

Participative games can also relax people, and help them feel more comfortable in a new setting.

REFLECTION - As a group leader, you have probably used a variety of "ice-breakers" or warm-up activities beyond those which have been described here.

Briefly record a few of the ones which have worked best for you. You may want to share these with others to compile your own "handbook" of methods to help members of a new group become acquainted and begin to develop group cohesiveness.

1. _____

_____

2. _____

_____

3. _____

_____

Other sources for ice-breakers and warm-ups are:

Forbess-Greene, S. (1980). *The encyclopedia of icebreakers: Structured Activities that warmup, motivate, challenge, acquaint and energize.* San Diego, CA.: Pfeiffer.

Warren, N. Associates Inc. (1992). *The warmups manual, Vol II. Toronto: Learnxs Press.*

A closing word on ice-breakers

Remember that people are unfamiliar with each other at the start of a new group. That is presumably why you are thinking about "ice-breakers", but it also means that the level of willingness to take risks will be low. Activities which would not seem the least bit threatening in the third session will promote much anxiety in the first. A guideline is to try to keep the anxiety level "optimal", meaning that there is enough challenge in the activity to get the "juices" flowing, without being so stressful that participants are immobilized and turned off. Obviously, the decision will need to be based on what you know (or assume you know) about your group members. Since you may be making assumptions based on little information, watch the group's reaction to your ice-breaker carefully, and respond to real resistance by letting go. The key-word here is "permission" — encourage group members always to make their own decisions based on their individual level of comfort — but at the same time encourage them to try something new before they decide to opt out.

Clarifying Expectations:
Setting Group Goals And Developing Commitment To The Task And The Team

Often, the content of the "getting acquainted" activities may be used as starting point for assessing the expectations of members for the group's work (ie: the focus of sub-group discussions can be "our hopes and concerns regarding our work as a group").

As group members enter in the "Forming" phase, their interests are individually-oriented ("what's in it for me?"). Acknowledging this as a legitimate concern, and even designing in an activity which allows the expression of such individual goals, allows members to examine what they have in common, and to begin to define group goals. Meshing individual and group goals is one of the most important facilitation challenges in the early (and ongoing) life of a group.

If you have assessed needs prior to the first group meeting, a summary of the data which you have collected, presented back to the group during the first session, can also initiate preliminary goal setting activities.

A design which works well is to begin by having participants express their personal wants, needs and questions in the ice-breaker activity, or through a summary of the needs assessment results. You can follow this by presenting participants with a summary of your goals for the group's work, or your understanding of its mandate. You then will want to examine and negotiate any discrepancies between your expectations and those of the group. This leads naturally to a goal-setting discussion which may produce an actual list of priorities, and a time-line for their accomplishment.

The key point to remember is that the more people are personally invested in the task focus, the greater will be their commitment and motivation.

Therefore, if people have been asked to join your group, or if the group's task has been mandated by someone other than the members, this will need to be well discussed. Members need to understand the group's significance to them in terms of their own interests. It is better to have people drop out of the group at this point, if their concerns cannot be addressed, than to mislead them regarding the group's purpose, or have them withdraw either psychologically or physically once work is underway.

Finally, goals are never finite and appropriate for all time. A maturely functioning group continually reassesses its goals and procedures, and makes changes as required.

Setting useful goals with a group is an activity which is often talked about, but rarely achieved. There are many factors which can block this process: "hidden agendas" (unexpressed goals) of the leader or group members; lack of clarity regarding expectations of others; differing wants/needs among group members; "political" pressures from a community or organization, to name just a few.

The following framework can be used to help a group set goals which are flexible, realistic, and representative of all members' interests — we call them "**S.M.A.R.T. GOALS**".

A Guideline For Setting S.M.A.R.T. Group Goals

SHARED: represents a meshing of individual and group or organization needs, and therefore generates commitment and "ownership". Goals must be understandable, desirable, challenging and believable in order to promote genuine interest.

MEASURABLE: specifically answers the question: "how will we know when we've accomplished the goal?" The answer is expressed in terms of the intended outcomes.

ACHIEVABLE: a goal which is within our capacity to accomplish (we have both the responsibility and the authority to tackle this project; it is within our control)

REALISTIC: we have the skills, time and resources to accomplish this goal (may imply deciding on short and long-term objectives)

TIME-PHASED: planned to be tackled in incremental steps, within specifically allocated time periods. Goals must be flexible and periodically reassessed for validity, given changing circumstances over time.

S.M.A.R.T. goals result from group discussion in which every member's ideas and concerns are heard. In the end, not all ideas will be used. Unless everyone feels that s/he can at least live with the resulting decisions, the group will lose the commitment of those members who are not on board. In the long-run it is worth the extra time it may take to ensure a sense of ownership for task goals by everyone in the group.

REFLECTION - Here is an opportunity to assess the goals you may have set with your selected group.

First, list the group's top-priority goals. Then rate each one individually, using the S.M.A.R.T. goal criteria. In addition, jot a few observations you have made for assessing these goals.

My group's top priority goals:

1. _____

2. _____

3. _____

S.M.A.R.T. CHART

	How does the goal rank?	What are the indicators
Shared	1___2___3___4___5 not great terrific	
Measurable	1___2___3___4___5 not great terrific	
Achievable	1___2___3___4___5 not great terrific	
Realistic	1___2___3___4___5 not great terrific	
Time-phased	1___2___3___4___5 not great terrific	

Question: What do you and your group need to do to ensure that you are working towards S.M.A.R.T. goals?

_____
_____
_____

Defining Your Role As Group "Facilitator"

One of the most important tasks of the forming phase of group development is to clarify expectations regarding the roles people will perform in the group.

Whether or not the roles are formally differentiated (ie: secretary, treasurer, etc.) each member will need to know clearly what is expected of him/her and of others. Early in the group's life it is the role of the designated leader which is potentially most confusing, and generally of most interest to group members.

You may choose to introduce your role as "facilitator" by stating that you expect to provide a very active and involved form of leadership initially, with the intention that your activity will decrease as group members take over the various leadership functions.

Be aware at all times that your behaviour serves as a model for effective group behaviour, and that, initially, you will have a great deal of influence on the developing norms of the group.

Following are some guidelines which may be helpful:

Your appearance

It is important that your choice of clothing reflect a sense of "professional-ism" without being overly formal. It may be useful to find out about what the norms of the group are likely to be, and then try to be reasonably consistent with these in your choice.

What you decide to wear will never be as noticeable as during the first meeting, when impressions are being formed. As the group progresses, and members come to value your contributions, your appearance will have less of an impact.

Learn first names as quickly as possible.

This reflects an interest in group members as individuals, and allows you to address people personally. Your use of members' names will also assist them in learning each others', and in this way generally contribute to the cohesiveness of the group.

You will find that early in the life of the group is it acceptable, even for the leader, to forget names and asked to be reminded. You may wish to incorporate a name-game into the introductory activities to help with this process.

Listen attentively, and respond to comments directly and seriously.

The facilitator is the primary "model" for group norms and behaviour during the early sessions. If s/he demonstrates enthusiastic, respectful responses to group members' contributions, they will do so more readily with one another.

The final and key issue is one of CONGRUENCE.

No matter how skillful or knowledgeable you are as a facilitator, your words will mean nothing if they are not supported by behaviour which is congruent with the theories and practices you are espousing. This does not imply that you have to be faultless. The most potent strength that a facilitator can offer a group is his or her genuine vulnerability. If you are prepared to admit that you are less than perfect, and that you may even have something to learn, others will also be more open and honest in their presentation of themselves. In the end, there is nothing more essential in developing a productive working environment in a group. ❖

Print Resources and Films

Print Resources

Dimock, H. (1986). *Factors in Working With Groups: Planning group development 2nd ed.* North York, Ont.: Captus Press.

Francis, D. & Young, D. (1979). *Improving work groups: A practical manual for team building.* San Diego, CA.: University Associates.

Hackman, J.R. (Ed.)(1990). *Groups that work (and those that don't): Creating conditions for effective teamwork.* San Francisco, CA.: Jossey-Bass.

Hersey, P. and Blanchard, K. (1990). *Management of organizational behaviour.* 2nd ed. Englewood Cliffs, N.J.: Prentice Hall.

Ingalls, J. (1973). *A trainer's guide to andragogy.* Waltham, MA.: Data Education.

Johnson, D. (1972). *Reaching out.* Englewood Cliffs, N.J.: Prentice-Hall.

Johnson, D. & Johnson, F. (1975). *Joining together: group theory and group skills.* Englewood Cliffs, N.J.: Prentice-Hall.

Lakey, B. N.d. *Meeting facilitation: The no magic method.* Philadelphia, PA.: New Society Publishers.

Miles, M. (1981). *Learning to work in groups.* 2nd ed. New York, N.Y.: Teachers College Press.

Schindler-Rainman, E. & Lippitt, R. (with Cole, J.) (1977). *Taking your meetings out of the doldrums.* La Jolla, CA.: University Associates.

Tuckman, B. (1965). *Developmental sequence in small groups.* Psychological Bulletin, 63, (6).

Films

1. "*Meetings, Bloody Meetings*"; Video Arts — approx. 30 minutes; available from International Telefilm, or the Ontario Ministry of Tourism and Recreation Resource Centre. A humorous look at the various problems and possibilities of chairing a meeting.

2. "*Team-building: Making the Task the Boss*" (18 minutes); available from McGraw-Hill. A graphic illustration of how "hidden agendas" can prevent a team from functioning cohesively, with concrete suggestions about how to help a group begin to work together towards shared goals.

GROUP DEVELOPMENT and FACILITATIVE LEADERSHIP

Phases of Group Development
(needs of group members)

Role of the Facilitator

Over time . . . .

Terminating the group's work

ADJOURNING

▷ Creates apprehension, minor crisis

▷ Regression in maturity level

▷ Needing help in saying "good-bye"

DELEGATING / SEPARATING

▷ Supporting, letting go

▷ Adjusting own leadership style

▷ Helping group deal with termination issues

Functioning as an effective group

PERFORMING

▷ Working productively toward shared goals

▷ Problem solving and decision-making

▷ Open communication, trust, respect

▷ Dealing with conflict

SUPPORTING

▷ Offering own resources, ideas

▷ Sharing the leadership role

Managing conflict, establishing "ground rules"

NORMING

▷ Resolving control concerns

▷ Establishing group agreement

▷ Catharsis, "honeymoon"

▷ Being available for one-to-one consultation/coaching

▷ Smoothing the interface between the group & the organization or community

---

Dealing with issues of power and control

STORMING

▷ Consolidating influence

▷ Confronting dependency on leader

▷ Conflict among group members
▷ Work level low

COACHING

▷ Surfacing issues, legitimizing concerns

▷ Facilitating communication, managing conflict

▷ Inviting input and feedback, sharing control

▷ Expecting and accepting tension

Developing a positive working environment

FORMING

▷ Becoming oriented

▷ Developing commitment

▷ Needing direction

▷ Wanting to be accepted, included

DIRECTING

▷ Climate setting

▷ Clarifying roles, expectations

▷ Defining goals, providing structure

▷ Group building

CREDITS: Model by Marilyn Laiken (1985); graphic design, Jeff Solway (1988); "phases of group development" headings, Bruce Tuckman (1965); "role of the facilitator" headings, K. Blanchard (1985)

3

STORMING PHASE

?

REFLECTION - Think about an on-going group, either recently, or in the past, which has felt difficult to work with. It could be the group which you described in your original case at the start of this manual.

Describe briefly what has been problematic.

_____

_____

Did the group which you described sound anything like this?...

The group has been working together for several weeks or months. Things have been rolling along. The members now feel comfortable with each other, and everyone is clear about the task at hand (or so you thought!). Recently, though, there's been tension in the ranks. Members can't seem to agree on anything without lengthy discussions, often resulting in no decision. People have started skipping meetings, and those who come, often arrive late. They've even started complaining about how you run the meetings, making side comments about "getting nowhere" while you're talking, and generally being disruptive in ways which you hadn't noticed previously.

Side bar conversations

Your first thought might be "this group is falling apart — I guess I must be doing something wrong". It's natural to feel some responsibility for the situation, since you have been providing most of the leadership to this point.

You might respond by sitting with this worry, hoping that the climate in the group will change on its own. Alternately, you might attempt to "lighten up" group meetings by suggesting a social activity, or a change of format. In any case, you will probably feel the need to do something, since you are, after all, the designated leader. The problem is that any changes which you suggest get rejected almost immediately, and no one else seems to be able to influence the direction of the group any more successfully.

It is likely that the group is in its "Storming" Phase of development. The good news is that if you can help the group weather this phase skilfully, members will become much more competent at handling conflict constructively in the future, and the group will become cohesive and effective in ways which at this point seem like an unrealistic fantasy!

But first, let's examine this phase in more detail — so that you will recognize it when it's happening, and understand its importance to the group's overall development.

THE STORMING PHASE

How do I recognize it?

Once members have become comfortable in the work setting, they are willing to take more risks with each other. People begin to offer their opinions and ideas more readily, and in so doing, try to influence the direction of the group.

Power and control is the key issue at this point. Up until this time, the group leader has exerted the greatest influence on the group, and members have accepted and most probably appreciated the structure and direction provided.

However, just as a two year old child or a teenager needs to separate to some extent from parental control, the maturing group needs to begin to direct its own process. Thus, the designated leader is challenged, and a "leadership vacuum" is created. Members may decide that they don't like the format in which the group has been operating, or they want to change the locale for meetings. Sometimes they will make these decisions without consulting the designated leader, and inform him or her after the fact.

There is an effort on the part of various group members to fill this vacuum by attempting to influence the decision making. The group may become polarized by a sub-group which wants to control the process, and another sub-group which wants to prevent the take-over. Conflicts among members become more common, as people begin to openly express their differences. As a result, decisions are difficult to reach, and the climate is fraught with tension, frustration, and a sense of "spinning wheels" and accomplishing nothing.

It is at this point that the group may begin to display "symptoms" of the Storming Phase, such as not attending meetings, arriving late, and expressing dissatisfaction in various ways.

In a training session, this phase is often accompanied by people complaining about minor physical ailments, feeling "dragged out" and energyless, having headaches, and so on. No matter how this phase is acted out, the atmosphere is often "stormy" and uncomfortable, and little work is accomplished.

What do group members need?

The most important need of group members at this time is to be able to freely express their concerns about the group, and to be heard, both by the leader and by each other.

Members need help in recognizing that conflict is to be expected in any situation where humans are interacting on an on-going basis.

The conditions which will allow the group to handle constructively the conflicts which arise in the Storming Phase include:

A climate which feels supportive, cooperative and "safe";

The use of specific skills in communicating information accurately (more detail on this when we consider the role of the facilitator);

A group norm which supports recognizing similarities in opinions, as well as differences (work from a position of strength!);

A group norm which views controversy as valuable;

A willingness on the part of the group leader and members to deal with feelings as well as facts;

A willingness to respect and affirm the personal contributions of others, even when disagreeing with their ideas: now, more than ever, "put-downs" are not permitted!;

Defining conflicts as "our problem" — no allocation of blame to individual members.

If these conditions are cultivated from the beginning of the group's work together, conflicts will begin to surface more readily, and mechanisms will be in place for dealing with them.

REFLECTION - **All of us have attitudes about and reactions to conflict which have developed through our family backgrounds, and our experiences at school and at work. Take a few minutes to define your understanding of the term "conflict"...**

Contrary to what most people believe, there are some real benefits in dealing directly with conflict in a group:

- It can make the group aware of problems which need to be resolved.
- It can make for better decisions, by allowing the group to get out of "ruts".
- It can reduce nagging, day-to-day irritants.
- It can deepen interpersonal relationships, and add to the cohesiveness of the group.
- It can provide personal insights.
- It can be energizing. It stimulates creativity by highlighting differences in approaches.
- It can increase confidence in the leader and the group to handle differences as they occur.

Can you think of other ways in which conflict can be useful? ...

In spite of all the benefits we have listed, most of us have been encouraged by our culture and role models to fear conflict, and to see it as something "nasty", to be avoided.

***REFLECTION* : List below all of the things which you consider to be negative about conflict: for instance. . .**

- It can open up "cans of worms"
- It may damage relationships

Others:

_____

_____

_____

_____

It is for all of the reasons you have outlined that people in groups tend to avoid dealing directly with conflictual issues.

Take a moment to think about your personal style of managing conflict.

The Thomas-Kilmann Conflict Mode Instrument (1977) may provide some useful insights for understanding conflict management styles (see "Print Resources" section). The authors outline five different styles which can be appropriate in different situations:

COMPETING (win/lose):
"might makes right"

Firm in pursuing personal goals; anxious to win; firm on own stance or viewpoint — believes it to be the "right answer".

AVOIDING (withdrawal):
"Leave well enough alone"

Feels that controversy is unpleasant, and to be avoided; tends to attribute responsibility for solving problems to others; often assumes "if you wait long enough, it will go away".

ACCOMMODATING (peace at all costs):
"Kill them with kindness"

Stresses the areas on which there is agreement; feels it's important to keep people happy and comfortable; believes that dealing with conflicts often results in hurt feelings; not engaging in conflicts makes me a more likable person, soothing feelings helps to preserve relationships.

COMPROMISING (the middle ground):
"Split the difference"

Expresses a desire to barter — to give up some points in exchange for others; assumes that the two positions proposed are the only ones available.

COLLABORATING (win/win; problem-solving):
"Two heads are better than one"

Attempts to deal with all concerns which are blocking; seeks others' help in working out a solution; is concerned with getting issues out in the open; believes that the process of dealing with conflict can be a creative experience; has faith in people's ability to work through conflictual issues.

Although most of us would like to believe that our conflict management style is mainly "collaborative", it is more likely that we avoid or withdraw from conflict. Such thoughts as: "It's not really important enough to make a fuss"... or, "It will probably blow over in a day or two", are the kinds of rationale we use to avoid dealing with "messy" situations.

If, as a facilitator, you are not confronting conflicts in your group as often or as openly as you could, it is likely that group members will take their cue from you.

REFLECTION : How does your style of managing conflict help or hinder you in working with your group(s)?

In the Storming Phase, as in all phases of group development, the designated leader has a key role to play in modelling the behaviour which will be most helpful to the group. In this phase the primary requirement is an ability to confront conflict directly.

However, if you tend to avoid conflict, don't despair — there are some very specific skills and methods which you can use to help you deal with conflict more constructively. These methods can also be learned by members of your group — with your help!

What can the facilitator do?

The Storming Phase is the most challenging one for the designated leader. S/he is in the difficult position of feeling responsible for the group's progress, without being permitted by the members to have much influence on its decisions.

From the group's point of view, the task to be accomplished tends to take such high priority, that "maintenance" only occurs when the work has ground to a complete halt over some unresolved issue or conflict. At this point the discomfort of members may become so acute that it seems easier to disband the group than to deal with the concerns. More frequently, the group attempts to push on with its task, ignoring the unexpressed anger, confusion or apathy. Hence, the work takes twice the amount of time it would if members were more fully engaged, and the blockages dealt with.

There are two important roles which you can play as facilitator during the Storming Phase of group development:

1. helping members to communicate effectively; and,

2. conducting "process analysis and feedback" sessions with your group.

Each of these is explored in detail in the following sections.

The Role of the Facilitator
Helping Group Members To Communicate Effectively

The tendency in groups, because of their task orientation, and members' discomfort with conflict, is to want to resolve problems quickly — sometimes before they are fully understood. The result is that the group may end up solving the wrong problem, and the real issue will surface again at a later date. If members of your group have said something like "how is it that we always get stuck on the same issue?", your group may be experiencing this blockage.

Before people can begin to resolve conflicts with each other, it is important that they share a clear understanding of the problematic issues. The need here is to help group members deal with their emotional reactions, both to each other, and to the situation at hand, without necessarily resolving the problem at this point.

You do not need to be a therapist or psychologist to facilitate a group through this phase. Two basic sets of skills, modelled by you, and eventually learned by group members, will go a long way in clarifying communication during conflictual periods. These are:

Making yourself understood — communicating your own thoughts and feelings effectively; and,

Understanding others — listening *"actively"*.

Following are specific techniques to help you and your group members use these skills.

Helping Members Provide Information About Their Side Of The Issue, And Be Heard

The key phrases are:

"When you ..."

"I feel .../because ..."

"I want/need ..."

"When you..."
(providing feedback to others about their behaviour)

Be specific; use observable information instead of generalized statements (ie: " Are you aware that you interrupted me three times in the last sentence?", instead of, " You always interrupt me when I'm talking").

Use descriptive, verifiable facts, instead of evaluative statements (ie: " You have interrupted me three times in the last sentence", instead of, " you are a pushy person").

Ask permission to offer feedback, rather than imposing it (ie: I have some information for you about how your behaviour affected me in our meeting. Is this a good time to talk about it?").

When you *ask* someone if they are willing to hear how their behaviour affects you, they are more likely to listen, than if you simply start to " dump" it on them. If they are not presently ready, you might ask when would be a better time. If they say " never", you might discuss the consequences of that decision in terms of working together effectively. If none of these responses works, give up — but leave the door open for future possibilities.

"I Feel.../Because..."
(describing your own feelings and reactions clearly)

Use "I-statements" — this will prevent you from making attributions about other people. Also, it is difficult for others to argue with a statement you make about your own feelings.

Include the reason for your reaction, so that the other person will better understand your position.

"I Need Or Want..."
(acting assertively/asking for what you need)

You have a right to describe clearly and non-defensively your own wants and needs. They may not necessarily be met, but there's no chance of a positive reaction if others don't know what they are!

Here is an example of how the above would sound if combined in one statement:

"When you interrupt me repeatedly, as you have done twice in the last sentence," *(providing feedback)*

"I feel frustrated, because I think you're not interested in what I'm saying." *(I-statement/reason)*

"I would like you to let me finish a thought without cutting me off." *(my wants/needs)*

Helping Members Listen Actively To Each Other

The key skills are:
- Non-verbal ("perception-checking", and body posture)
- Verbal ("paraphrasing")

Active Listening Non-Verbally

1. Perception-checking:

checking your assumptions about the other's non-verbal cues (ie: " You seem upset today .. are you?")
- opens the door for further communication;
- helps you avoid making incorrect assumptions, and acting on them;
- helps the other person feel heard.

2. Listening Actively With Your Body:

- nodding, leaning into the conversation, maintaining eye contact, not allowing yourself to be distracted, etc.

NOTE: It is important to recognize that some non-verbal cues will vary in their meaning among different cultures. For instance, direct eye contact may indicate attentive listening to a Westerner, but may be a sign of disrespect to someone from an Eastern culture. Alerting your group members to these differences, or helping them express differences to one another if they exist in the group, will aid in the communication process.

Active Listening Verbally

"Paraphrasing" is one method of verbal active listening. Using your own words, you repeat your understanding of what the other person has said. You then check to ensure that what you heard is what was intended. Paraphrasing serves a number of purposes. It:
- helps the other person feel heard;
- allows for clarification of misunderstandings;
- slows down the action; takes the " heat" out of the discussion;
- helps to put you in the other person's shoes for a time.

Each of these methods requires practice in order to be used effectively. Initially, you may feel awkward as you experiment with them. As with any other skill, it becomes easier with repeated effort (remember how difficult it was when you were learning to ride your first bike?). As you and your group members practice these skills, the communication in your group will improve dramatically. Problems will not only be resolved, but they will stay resolved!

REFLECTION : Which situations in a group do you find most difficult to handle? What do you need to learn in order to deal with these situations more effectively?

The Role Of The Facilitator
Conducting Process Analysis And Feedback Sessions

You may find that interpersonal conflicts are not the only problems which arise in your group during the Storming Phase. Group members may become dissatisfied with the way the group is functioning, or with some of the decisions about goals which were made during an earlier period.

Although your job would be easier if members could express these concerns to the group as they arise, during the Storming Phase this is unlikely to happen without your help. Just as group leaders often tend to avoid conflict, so do other group members. Such openness needs to be consciously developed as a group norm. People need to learn ways of expressing their concerns which lead to a problem-solving, rather than a blaming stance.

Conducting " process analysis and feedback" sessions (more commonly referred to as " processing") will help to teach your group members these skills.

This method involves a periodic movement away from the " content" or topic of discussion, to focus on the " process", or how the discussion is being conducted, and the task accomplished.

The importance of processing is that it encourages members to begin collecting data and making recommendations which affect the on-going structure and functioning of the group. In this manner, the control begins to move out of the hands of the designated leader, and is shared by the group as a whole.

Processing can occur in two ways:

1. It can be done intermittently, as the group proceeds through its task.;

2. It can be scheduled. That is, it can occur during an agreed-upon time within a meeting, possibly part-way through or at the end of the session.

1. Intermittent Process Analysis

This is based on an agreed-upon ground rule which permits any member to comment on the work of the group as it proceeds. Usually this is not done unless there is something obviously blocking the group in its functioning. In this case, all group members act as "participant observers", participating in the group's task, while observing, and occasionally commenting on its "process". In so doing, members "heave out the garbage" whenever its odour is detected, rather than waiting for it to build up and bury the group!

An example of a process comment is: "I notice for the last half hour we've touched on four topics, and discussed none of them. Perhaps we need to have another look at our priorities." This may refocus the group's discussion, and allow members to continue their work more productively.

An equally powerful process comment is an expression of personal confusion. For example, "I've lost track of what we're doing now. Can we clarify the problem once again?". Often, this type of statement reflects the unspoken feelings of other members, who will be relieved that someone took the risk to say what was also bothering them.

Initially, process comments will need to be made by the group leader. At this time, s/he might use the opportunity to discuss the concept of "processing" with the group as a proposed norm for working together more effectively. As the group matures, members will begin to share the responsibility of calling a halt to the proceedings, and raising issues to be resolved whenever the group is bogged down.

2. Scheduled Process Analysis

In order to teach members "processing" skills, you may find it helpful to initiate a regular process analysis session as part of each group meeting. It need not take more than ten or fifteen minutes, if done on a regular basis — and will soon be regarded by members as an important "investment" in maintaining the health of the group.

Initially, it is wise to provide some structure for these sessions in order to introduce a relatively new concept. Less structure will be needed as members become proficient in their ability to both observe and discuss their observations in a constructive way.

Here are some suggestions for ways to structure your processing sessions. These are listed in order from the most highly structured to the least.

Post-meeting Reaction Forms

Post meeting reaction forms usually involve a paper and pencil questionnaire which is completed anonymously by each group member. The responses are then summarized by the facilitator or a small committee, and the results are presented back to the group for discussion.

Following is an example of a post-meeting reaction form which you might wish to use with your group.

A variation on this approach would be to ask the group members to construct their own form with questions which seem particularly relevant to them.

The data may be collected mid-way through the meeting, summarized at the break, and then presented back; or may be collected at the end of a session and presented back at the opening of the next meeting. A few minutes spent discussing any problematic issues which arise from the responses can help prevent them from reaching major, less resolvable proportions.

POST MEETING REACTION FORM

1. Generally, how did you feel about today's meeting?

1 . . . . . 2 . . . . . 3 . . . . . 4 5
very dissatisfied   very satisfied

2. What were the major strengths of the meeting?

. . . .

. . . .

3. Was there anything about the meeting which
you feel hindered our progress as a group today?

. . . .

. . . .

4. How could our next meeting be improved?

. . . .

. . . .

5. Any other comments?

. . . .

. . . .

. . . .

. . . .

Polls

A poll serves the same purpose as the post-meeting reaction form, but tends to be less time consuming, in that the information is summarized as it is collected, usually using a continuum format. This may be done on a flip-chart, posing such questions as:

POLL

1. How satisfied are you with how our group accomplished its tasks today?

   not satisfied   1____2____3____4____5   very satisfied

2. How satisfied are you with the way the group worked together?

   not satisfied   1____2____3____4____5   very satisfied

3. How satisfied are you with your participation in the group's work?

   not satisfied   1____2____3____4____5   very satisfied

Again, in this procedure, group members may choose to generate their own questions, and then respond to them. Responses are made individually by going around the room, with each member placing him or herself on each continuum, one by one. The group then examines the total picture for areas indicating a particular pattern, which is then discussed more fully.

This method represents a slightly higher level of risk than the written response sheet, as people are not able to remain anonymous in their responses. However, it can also lead to a more open and specific discussion, and is particularly helpful in raising concerns which participants may be harbouring about their own contribution to the group.

Group observers

This method for gathering information about the group's process requires greater skill on the part of group members, but can be an extremely effective approach in helping a group to examine its functioning in depth.

In this case, the group may decide to ask one or more members to stop participating in the discussion temporarily, and to watch and record notes on what is going on in the meeting. The observers then report a summary of their observations back to the group, which leads naturally into a discussion on blockages and how they might be resolved. Some areas upon which group observers might focus are: (from Dimock, 1985).

Climate (the atmosphere within the group)

- This can be physical (ie: lighting, seating arrangements etc.), or it can be emotional (ie: formal, informal, tense, accepting).

Participation, Involvement, Interaction

- This includes such factors as frequency of contribution; communication patterns (who talks to whom, and how often); and non-verbal communication.

Group Cohesion
- Is there evidence of team-work?
- Is there acceptance of and appreciation for individual differences?
- Do group members seem to enjoy working together?

Productivity/accomplishment of the task(s)

- Is the task understood by all?
- Do members seem challenged by the tasks in which they are involved?
- Is information shared and available when needed?
- What are the group's decision making procedures, and do they result in decisions which get implemented?
- Do group members seem satisfied with the results of the group's work?

Leadership Roles

- Is leadership shared, or does it seem to be the property of one person?
- What kinds of methods/behaviours are being used to influence group activities, or to help the group move forward in its work?

Following is a sample form to use in observing your group.

GROUP PROCESS OBSERVATION FORM

1. CLIMATE

    Physical: . . . .

    Emotional: . . . .

2. PARTICIPATION, INVOLVEMENT, INTERACTION:

    . . . .

    . . . .

3. GROUP COHESION:

    . . . .

    . . . .

4. PRODUCTIVITY:

    . . . .

    . . . .

5. LEADERSHIP ROLES:

    . . . .

    . . . .

Dimock (1985)

Guidelines For Observers In Collecting And Reporting Back Observations To The Group

To collect information:

- Ensure that all members have agreed to be observed, and have requested the type of feedback which would be most useful to them (they can help construct the observation areas or questions).

- Sit quietly in a position where all members are visible.

- Observe, but do not participate in the discussion, for a specified period of time (probably not more than 30 minutes).

- Take notes on agreed-upon areas, illustrating them with specific examples of behaviour which you have observed.

To report your observations to the group:

- Summarize your observations in a manner which is clear and concise — limit your feedback to those areas which seem most relevant to the group's needs.

- Your observations will be most useful to the group if they are specific, objectively stated (no judgments), supported by observed examples, and validated with the group (do they agree?). The guidelines for offering feedback constructively apply here.

- Do not argue about your observations with the group. Simply present your feedback as data to be discussed. If the group responds defensively, you may want to reexamine the way in which you presented the information. Finally, never forget that you too are a member of this group, and probably have been contributing to any of the problems which you have observed!

SUMMARY

There are a variety of methods for collecting information about your group. Some of those which have been described are: intermittent process analysis; post-meeting reaction forms and polls; and the use of group observers.

Whichever method you choose, the key point being made is that the effective group will develop a habit of regularly reflecting on its procedures, as well as ensuring its task accomplishment.

The methods in this section for facilitating a group through its Storming Phase can be summarized in one important " guideline" :

When all else fails, ask the group, " what's going on here?", and then be prepared to really listen to the response! ❖

Print Resources

Briggs Meyers, I. with Meyers, P.B. (1980). *Gifts differing*. Palo Alto, CA.: Consulting Psychologists Press.

Crum, T.F. (1899). *The magic of conflict*. New York,N.Y.: Touchstone Books.

Dimock, H. (1985). *How to analyze and evaluate group growth*. North York, Ont.: Captus Press.

Dimock, H. (1985). *How to observe your group*. North York, Ont.: Captus Press.

Fisher, R. & Brown, S. (1988). *Getting together: Building a relationship that gets to yes*. Boston,MA.: Houghton Mifflin.

Fisher, R. & Brown. (1989). *Getting together: Building relationships as we negotiate*. New York,N.Y.: Penguin.

Fordyce, J.K. & Weil, R. (1971). *Managing with people*. Reading, MA.: Addison-Wesley.

Jandt, F.E. (1985). *Win-Win negotiating: Turning conflict into agreement*. New York,N.Y.: John Wiley & Sons.

Johnson, B. (1992). *Polarity management*. Amherst, MA.: HRD Press.

Thomas, K.W. & Kilmann, R. (1977). Developing a forced-choice measure of conflict handling behaviour: The mode instrument. *Educational and Psychological Measurement, 37, 309-325*.

Films

1) "*More Bloody Meetings*", Video Arts (approx. 30 min.); available from International Telefilm or the Ontario Ministry of Tourism and Recreation (Resource Centre).

A humorous treatment of the "human side of meetings" — how to handle conflict and help keep the group focussed on the task at hand.

2) "*The Art of Negotiating*"; available from McGraw-Hill or Barr Films.

An instructive guide to negotiating in a way which meets the needs of all parties. Is focussed on the art of bargaining with individuals rather than on reaching consensus within a group, but contains some transferable principles.

3) "*Twelve Angry Men*"; a feature film (approx. 2 hours, black and white) available from your local video rental store.

The film is dated — Henry Fonda, who stars, is in his twenties! However, it provides an excellent model for the leadership of a group in conflict. In this case, the group is a jury deciding on a murder sentence.

4) "*From No to Yes*"; available from International Telefilm, (approx. 30 min.)

An excellent demonstration of the basic skills needed to manage disagreement in a group towards "win-win" solutions.

GROUP DEVELOPMENT and FACILITATIVE LEADERSHIP

Phases of Group Development
(needs of group members)

Role of the Facilitator

Terminating the group's work

ADJOURNING

▷ Creates apprehension, minor crisis
▷ Regression in maturity level
▷ Needing help in saying "good-bye"

DELEGATING / SEPARATING

▷ Supporting, letting go
▷ Adjusting own leadership style
▷ Helping group deal with termination issues

Functioning as an effective group

PERFORMING

▷ Working productively toward shared goals
▷ Problem solving and decision-making
▷ Open communication, trust, respect
▷ Dealing with conflict

SUPPORTING

▷ Offering own resources, ideas
▷ Sharing the leadership role

Managing conflict, establishing "ground rules"

NORMING

▷ Resolving control concerns
▷ Establishing group agreement
▷ Catharsis, "honeymoon"

▷ Being available for one-to-one consultation/coaching
▷ Smoothing the interface between the group & the organization or community

Dealing with issues of power and control

STORMING

▷ Consolidating influence
▷ Confronting dependency on leader
▷ Conflict among group members
▷ Work level low

COACHING

▷ Surfacing issues, legitimizing concerns
▷ Facilitating communication, managing conflict
▷ Inviting input and feedback, sharing control
▷ Expecting and accepting tension

Developing a positive working environment

FORMING

▷ Becoming oriented
▷ Developing commitment
▷ Needing direction
▷ Wanting to be accepted, included

DIRECTING

▷ Climate setting
▷ Clarifying roles, expectations
▷ Defining goals, providing structure
▷ Group building

Over time...

CREDITS: Model by Marilyn Laiken (1985); graphic design, Jeff Solway (1988); "phases of group development" headings, Bruce Tuckman (1965); "role of the facilitator" headings, K. Blanchard (1985)

4

NORMING
& PERFORMING PHASES

NORMING PHASE
A bridge to performing effectively

How do I recognize it, and what do members need?

Although the Storming Phase of group development described in the previous chapter is fraught with discomfort and indecision, eventually the tide breaks. As issues are surfaced and discussed, and the group begins to trust that the facilitator will indeed allow members to take more control, they begin to relax with the process. "Norms", or standards of operating, are redefined by the group. They may look very different from those originally proposed during the Forming Phase.

Members may decide that from now on their meetings will last only two hours, instead of three, and that the chair will be rotated, rather than resting in the hands of one person. They may review the locale for their meetings and suggest a change. Or they may discuss ways in which they will behave differently during sessions (eg: only one person talks at a time, the group gives every idea a hearing before deciding on one, etc.).

Norms vary from group to group. The key guideline, however, is that the decisions in this phase are made by the group, and are influenced as little as possible by the designated leader.

The more the facilitator can stay out of the way during this discussion, the more likely the group will move through the phase quickly, and on to the Performing Phase — where, once again, your opinions will be welcomed. Sometimes the group will help you in this task by having the discussion at a time when you are not present (this is otherwise known as "throwing out the leader"!). They will then inform you of their decisions, and hope that you will go along.

What can the facilitator do?

At this point, you will find it most effective to flow with the group's direction, even if the decisions being made don't seem like the best choice to you. Remember that a fair decision which has everyone's commitment is far better than an "excellent" decision which is never implemented!

Obviously, you will want to intervene if the proposals contravene some important guideline of which the group may not be aware. However, if you have been honest with the group from the start, it is unlikely that members will propose anything that will cause you problems. In fact, they don't really want to get rid of you — they just want to share some of your power and control over the group.

Reminding yourself at this point that the group is experiencing a natural and healthy phase in its development towards maturity will help you to remain non-defensive. That is probably the biggest challenge during this phase, as many of the group's decisions will be, by necessity, a direct reversal of your original proposals. (Think about the teenager who shows up at the home of his middle-aged, professional parents, sporting a "Mohawk" hair style!).

Another important challenge for you as facilitator is not to panic and take control. A leap of faith is required here, but your experience will prove that the group really does know what it needs, and will find a way through its problems.

There are several dangers in taking control at this stage. The reversion is likely to generate intense hostility which will probably be directed at you. Presuming you are successful, the group might revert to a dependent mode, and either remain there, or "storm" indefinitely. Neither of these is a fate one would wish upon any facilitator or group!

A useful action, instead, would be to find support for yourself, someone to talk with who has had a similar experience, and who can reassure you that this, too, will pass.

The "Honeymoon"

Once the group has reached a decision about how it will operate in the future, there tends to be an almost cathartic sense of relief ("Well, we made it through this one intact — aren't we a great group!"). There will often follow a tension-releasing celebrational atmosphere. In a residential setting, this is often when the all-night party occurs.

Movement to the next phase results from group members recognizing that there is still work to accomplish — just as after the wedding honeymoon, the couple eventually returns home to begin "real life" in their marriage.

REFLECTION - Imagine that your group has survived the Storming Phase, and is returning from its "honeymoon" ready to work as a high-performing, mature team.

Take a few minutes to create for yourself a "vision" which describes how your group would function if it were the best it could be. What are the elements of your vision?

- How do members treat each other?

- How does the group deal with conflict?

- How do people feel about the work they are doing?

- How do you know that this group is effective in its task?

- What is your role, and how do members treat you?

GROUP DEVELOPMENT and FACILITATIVE LEADERSHIP

Phases of Group Development
(needs of group members)

Role of the Facilitator

Over time.....

Terminating the group's work

ADJOURNING

▷ Creates apprehension, minor crisis

▷ Regression in maturity level

▷ Needing help in saying "good-bye"

DELEGATING / SEPARATING

▷ Supporting, letting go

▷ Adjusting own leadership style

▷ Helping group deal with termination issues

Functioning as an effective group

PERFORMING

▷ Working productively toward shared goals

▷ Problem solving and decision-making

▷ Open communication, trust, respect

▷ Dealing with conflict

SUPPORTING

▷ Offering own resources, ideas

▷ Sharing the leadership role

Managing conflict, establishing "ground rules"

NORMING

▷ Resolving control concerns

▷ Establishing group agreement

▷ Catharsis, "honeymoon"

▷ Being available for one-to-one consultation/coaching

▷ Smoothing the interface between the group & the organization or community

---

Dealing with issues of power and control

STORMING

▷ Consolidating influence

▷ Confronting dependency on leader

▷ Conflict among group members

▷ Work level low

COACHING

▷ Surfacing issues, legitimizing concerns

▷ Facilitating communication, managing conflict

▷ Inviting input and feedback, sharing control

▷ Expecting and accepting tension

Developing a positive working environment

FORMING

▷ Becoming oriented

▷ Developing commitment

▷ Needing direction

▷ Wanting to be accepted, included

DIRECTING

▷ Climate setting

▷ Clarifying roles, expectations

▷ Defining goals, providing structure

▷ Group building

CREDITS: Model by Marilyn Laiken (1985); graphic design, Jeff Solway (1988); "phases of group development" headings, Bruce Tuckman (1965); "role of the facilitator" headings, K. Blanchard (1985)

PERFORMING PHASE

How do I recognize it?

It is likely that the elements of the "vision" you have created describe a group in its "Performing" Phase.

Following are some of the attributes of a mature group — one which is performing optimally in achieving its goals and in maintaining an atmosphere where members want to invest their energies.

> The atmosphere tends to be informal, comfortable, relaxed. People are involved and interested. There are no signs of boredom.

> Everyone participates to some extent in the discussion, which generally remains pertinent to the task of the group. If it gets off-track, someone brings it back quickly and effectively.

> The goals of the group are well understood and accepted by members. They will have been formulated through open discussion which has taken into account all members' needs and ideas. There is evident commitment to the final results.

> Group members listen to each other. There are few interruptions, and ideas are built upon, rather than negated. People do not seem to be afraid of appearing foolish by asking a "dumb question", or putting forth a creative thought.

> There is disagreement. The group shows no signs of wanting to avoid conflict or smooth over dissension. Disagreements are not suppressed or overridden by premature group action. The reasons are carefully examined, and the group seeks to resolve the issue, rather than to dominate the dissenter.

> Sometimes there are basic disagreements which cannot be resolved. The group finds it possible to live with them, accepting them, but not permitting them to block its efforts. Under some conditions, action will be deferred to permit further study of an issue. On other occasions, where the disagreements cannot be resolved and action is necessary, it will be taken — but with caution, and recognition that there may be a need for future reconsideration of the problem.

Decisions are made with the direct involvement of those who will be responsible for their implementation. Sometimes this will be the entire group, sometimes a sub-committee, and at other times it may involve only the designated leader. However, the decision about who makes the decision will be the responsibility of the whole group. Formal voting as a method of decision making is used minimally; the group does not accept a simple majority as a proper basis for action.

Feedback is frequent, frank and relatively comfortable. There is little evidence of personal attack, either openly or in a hidden fashion. Negative feedback, or criticism, is oriented towards removing an obstacle which faces the group and prevents it from getting the job done.

People are free in expressing their feelings as well as their ideas, both on the task and on the group's operation. There is little " pussyfooting" and there are few "hidden agendas". Everybody appears to understand how everyone else feels about a matter under discussion.

When action is taken, clear assignments are made and accepted. Decisions not only are implemented effectively, but also are evaluated once the action has been taken, so that the group can fully enjoy its successes, and learn from its mistakes.

Chairpersons or group leaders do not dominate the group, nor does the group unduly defer to them. Their leadership style is appropriate to the situation. In fact, the leadership shifts from time to time, depending on the circumstances. Different members, because of their knowledge or experience, feel free to offer their resources. Members' strengths are recognized and utilized to the benefit of the entire group.

There is little evidence of a struggle for power as the group operates. The issue is not who is in control, but how to get the job done.

The group is self-conscious about its own operation. Frequently, it will stop to examine how well it is doing, or what may be interfering with its functioning. The problem may be a matter of procedure, or an individual whose behaviour is blocking the group. Whatever it is, the issue is openly discussed until a solution is found.

(Based on notes taken from Douglas McGregor's " *The Human Side of Enterprise*", 1960)

What do members need during the Performing Phase?

If a group matches the description previously outlined, it is considered a "mature group".

Members will need the resources to work most effectively. They also need the freedom to function as autonomously as possible.

Since there is an increased level of trust, and more data available to the group through direct and honest communication, the work level is generally high. Although conflicts may slow task accomplishment, the group is able to resolve these quickly and move on. Since the group processes its functioning regularly, the "wheel-spinning" discussions of the Storming Phase rarely occur. Group goals are shared, explicit, flexible and promote high interest among all members.

What can the facilitator do?

This is probably the most important question in this phase, as the phase presents a new and unfamiliar challenge to the facilitator. The group no longer needs you as its "leader". Although members will now view you as a valuable resource in terms of your knowledge and opinions, your input is as valued as that of any other member — no more influential, no less.

Since the leadership roles are being shared by members of the group, your role in facilitating the group's process lessens in importance. At this stage, it is probably more helpful to the group if you take increasingly less responsibility for both the process and the content of the discussion.

However, there is still some concrete leadership which you can provide in other areas:

- You can continue to support and encourage the group; feedback from you periodically will still be welcomed and valued.

- You can be available to individual members for one-to-one consultation and coaching.

- You can serve as a "boundary buffer" to the group, keeping disruptions out, and ensuring that needed resources (whether they be people, information, materials or funds) are accessible. You can also perform a "liaison" role between the group and others with whom they may need to interact.

- You can ask the group what they need from you, or what role they would like you to play.

- Finally, since the key role of the group in this phase is to be involved in problem solving and decision making, you can help provide specific systems and methods which will develop members' skills in this area. This can be accomplished through separate training sessions, or during on-going meetings, as members work steadily towards accomplishing their goals.

Following is some information which you may find useful in providing groups with a systematic approach to problem solving.

Systematic Problem Solving

Step 1: Locate and define the problem

This involves a clarification of the issue being discussed.

Often groups begin to solve a problem before everyone has a clear understanding of the focus for the discussion. Or else the group is trying to resolve what turns out to be a symptom, rather than the root problem. The result is that the group will eventually need to recycle back to this step — probably after much unnecessary frustration!

One way of defining the problem is to have the group imagine a desired future state (the "target"); and then to examine where it is in reality (the "situation"). The problem is then defined in terms of the gap (how do we move from where we are now to where we want to be on this issue? What is the "path"?).

Questions which a group might ask itself at this stage are:

- Does everyone here need to be involved in the problem solving? Is everyone interested in investing his or her energy in this problem? If the answer is "no", you might consider sub-grouping, and having people work on different issues. If most people don't seem interested, the goal being tackled by the problem solving session should be reconsidered.

- Do we have the necessary information/resources to continue to work on the problem at this point? If not, how can we get what we need?

- Do we have control over this issue, and the authority to act on our ideas? If not, the group may be satisfied with making recommendations to someone else, but this should be clarified up-front.

- Is the task manageable in the time which is available? If not, it may be possible to determine sub-goals. Otherwise the goal needs to be reassessed in terms of its appropriateness for this group.

Step 2: Analyze the problem

Once the group is clear about its task, it is important to examine the issue more closely.

One way of doing this is to identify all of the forces which may be acting on the problem, by listing the factors which are influencing the group in reaching its goals.

A useful technique for this purpose is called " *Force Field Analysis*" (Kurt Lewin, 1947). The following steps summarize this method.

A. From your shared understanding of the problem to be solved, define one or two clear, realistically attainable goals.

B. Identify both the " driving" and the " restraining" forces which are either promoting or preventing movement towards each goal.

C. Analyze the forces by indicating which ones are " givens", and cannot be changed, and by deciding on the relative strength of each force.

D. Systematically "brainstorm" ways of strengthening the driving forces, and reducing the restraining forces (see next step in the sequence).

Step 3: Generate multiple solutions

One of the blocks groups often encounter to effective problem solving is a premature closure on solutions. One member will make a proposal, and either the group gets excited about it and begins to plan for its implementation, thereby precluding hearing other potentially good ideas; or the group squashes it, in which case the member whose idea it was feels " put down".

One way of avoiding this is to separate the idea generation from the evaluation phases. A method for doing this is called "brainstorming".

The purpose of brainstorming is to help group members suspend critical judgment, and thus enhance their creativity.

The "ground-rules" for brainstorming are:

- Generate as many ideas as possible from all sources.
- Wild ideas are encouraged — people will build on them.
- Quantity, rather than quality is the goal at this point.
- All ideas are recorded and numbered, preferably on a flip chart, or black or white board, for easy reference later.
- No evaluation of any kind, verbal or non-verbal, is permitted at this point!

Note: groups may need reminding about the last item, as quick evaluation of ideas comes naturally to most of us.

Step 4: Reach a decision

The method of decision making which is used in the group will need to be decided up-front, and should be appropriate to the situation.

Options can vary between:

- agreement (consensus) of the entire group
- majority vote
- minority of group members
- averaging of individual opinions of group members
- member with the most expertise
- member with the most authority after a group discussion of the issues
- member with the most authority without a group discussion.

Each of these methods has its own advantages and disadvantages, usually involving a choice between expediency and the commitment of members to the final outcome.

The important "guidelines" in deciding which method to use are:

- Ensure that the method is discussed and agreed to by the group members, with an understanding of the implications of their choice.

- Those who will be directly affected by the decision, or who will be directly involved in its implementation, need to have input into the decision in order to feel committed to it.

The decision about method should also take into account:

- The phase of development in which the group is located (a less mature group will have more trouble reaching consensus decisions);

- Your style as facilitator, and what you feel comfortable with;

- The norms of the group or the organization of which it is part.

If your group attempts to make a consensus decision, the following "tips" will help.

Guidelines For Making Consensus Decisions

"CONSENSUS" is a decision making process for making full use of the available resources, and for resolving problems creatively. Since this method takes everyone's concerns and ideas into account, it tends to ensure strong "ownership" for, and therefore commitment to the resulting decision.

However, consensus is difficult to reach. Therefore, complete unanimity is not the goal, since it is rarely achieved. The intention of consensus is that each individual be able to "live with" the decision, on the basis of its logic and feasibility.

In attempting to achieve consensus:

Encourage members to avoid arguing for their own position. Present ideas as logically and clearly as possible, and then allow the group to work with them.

Do not assume that someone must win and someone must lose when the discussion reaches a stalemate. Instead, look for the next most acceptable alternative to all members.

Do not change your mind simply to avoid conflict and reach agreement. When agreement seems to come too quickly, be suspicious. Explore the reasons, and be sure that everyone has been heard and accepts the solution for basically similar reasons.

Avoid conflict reducing techniques such as majority vote, averages, coin-flips and bargaining. When a dissenting member finally agrees, don't feel that s/he must be rewarded by having his/her own way at some later point.

Differences are natural, and to be expected. Seek them out, and try to involve everyone in the decision making process. Disagreements can help provide for a wider range of ideas, and an ultimately better solution. Encourage a variety of ideas with methods such as "brainstorming".

Step 5: Plan for action

Too often, groups are so delighted about finally having reached a decision, that members will leave before they have created a concrete action plan for how that decision will be implemented.

If you want to ensure that a decision is carried, do not end the meeting until you have agreed on:

- What will be done?
- Who will be doing it?
- When will the action be taken?
- Which materials and resources are needed?
- How will you know if your plan has been successful?

Finally, the group should be encouraged to forecast any consequences of the intended actions — and perhaps to formulate some contingency plans to deal with them.

Step 6: Implement the plan

Go for it! Identify checkpoints to ensure that you are on target and that deadlines are being met.

If you are not on target, identify the problems, and adjust the action plan accordingly.

Step 7: Evaluate and replan

Identify a date when the group can convene to evaluate the success of the project. If successful — congratulations!

If not successful, why not? Begin again with **Step 1. Locate and define the problem.**

In summary, following is the above sequence outlined in a handout format. If each group member has a copy, it will provide a "map" for effective group problem solving and decision making.

SYSTEMATIC PROBLEM SOLVING

*S*ITUATION   *T*ARGET/GOAL   *P*ATH

Where are we now?   Where do we want to be?   How do we get there?

1. Locate and define the problem

Check understandings, perceptions, agreements, disagreements and involvement.

State a specific goal.

Gather information necessary to work on the problem

2. Analyze the problem

Which forces are at work (facilitating and restraining)

     a) in the immediate situation?
     b) in terms of the broader context?

3. Generate multiple solutions

One method is "brainstorming":
     Phase 1: suggest ideas non-evaluatively
     Phase 2: test feasibility (evaluate alternatives)

4. Reach a decision

Use a method appropriate to the situation.

5. Plan for action

Assign roles (who)
Materials and resources needed (what)
Sequence in time (when)
Forcast consequences of intended action
(may imply contingency plans)

6. Implement the plan

7. Evaluate and replan

Review appropriateness of goals.

PRINT RESOURCES

Aubrey, II, C.A. (1988). *Teamwork: Involving people in quality and productivity improvement.* Wisconsin, N.J.: ASQC Quality Press.

Buchholz, S. & Roth, T. (1987). *Creating the high performance team.* Rexdale, Ont.: Wiley.

Cooper S. & Heenan, C. (1980). *"Co-designing"* from *Preparing, designing and leading workshops: A humanistic approach.* Boston, MA.: CBI Publishing Co.

Craig, D. (1978). *Hip pocket guide to planning and evaluation.* San Diego, CA.: University Associates.

Dimock, H. (1986). *A simplified guide to program evaluation.* 2nd ed. Guelph, Ont.: University of Guelph.

Dimock, H. (1986). *How to plan staff training programs. 2nd ed. Guelph, Ont.: University of Guelph.*

Kraus, W. (1980). *Collaboration in organizations: Alternatives to hierarchy.* New York, N.Y.: McGraw Hill.

McGregor, D. (1960). *The human side of enterprise.* New York, N.Y.: McGraw-Hill.

Morgan, G. (1986). *Images of organization.* Beverley Hills, CA.: Sage Publications.

Morrow, A.J. (1969). *The practical theorist: The life and work of Kurt Lewin.* New York, N.Y.: Basic Books.

Peters, T. & Waterman, R. Jr. (1982). *In search of excellence.* New York, N.Y.: Harper and Row.

Serge, P. (1990). *The fifth discipline: The art and practice of the learning organization.* New York, N.Y.: Doubleday Currency.

Stewart, A. (1989). *Team entrepreneurship.* London: Sage.

Films

1) "*Creative Problem-solving*" (available from the Ontario Ministry of Tourism and Recreation — Resource Centre)

An entertaining examination of both individual and group creativity, and how it can be helped or hindered.

2) "*Try Again, and Succeed*" (available form M.T.R., as above)

A delightful, short, animated film which illustrates beautifully the concept of "facilitative leadership".

GROUP DEVELOPMENT and FACILITATIVE LEADERSHIP

Phases of Group Development
(needs of group members)

Role of the Facilitator

Terminating the group's work	**ADJOURNING** ▷ Creates apprehension, minor crisis ▷ Regression in maturity level ▷ Needing help in saying "good-bye"	**DELEGATING / SEPARATING** ▷ Supporting, letting go ▷ Adjusting own leadership style ▷ Helping group deal with termination issues
Functioning as an effective group	**PERFORMING** ▷ Working productively toward shared goals ▷ Problem solving and decision-making ▷ Open communication, trust, respect ▷ Dealing with conflict	**SUPPORTING** ▷ Offering own resources, ideas ▷ Sharing the leadership role
Managing conflict, establishing "ground rules"	**NORMING** ▷ Resolving control concerns ▷ Establishing group agreement ▷ Catharsis, "honeymoon"	▷ Being available for one-to-one consultation/coaching ▷ Smoothing the interface between the group & the organization or community
Dealing with issues of power and control	**STORMING** ▷ Consolidating influence ▷ Confronting dependency on leader ▷ Conflict among group members ▷ Work level low	**COACHING** ▷ Surfacing issues, legitimizing concerns ▷ Facilitating communication, managing conflict ▷ Inviting input and feedback, sharing control ▷ Expecting and accepting tension
Developing a positive working environment	**FORMING** ▷ Becoming oriented ▷ Developing commitment ▷ Needing direction ▷ Wanting to be accepted, included	**DIRECTING** ▷ Climate setting ▷ Clarifying roles, expectations ▷ Defining goals, providing structure ▷ Group building

Over time....

CREDITS: Model by Marilyn Laiken (1985); graphic design, Jeff Solway (1988); "phases of group development" headings, Bruce Tuckman (1965); "role of the facilitator" headings, K. Blanchard (1985)

ADJOURNING:

Helping A Group Which No Longer Needs To Meet

Bruce Tuckman has recently added a fifth phase to his theory of group development. He calls it "adjournment", and refers to it as a "minor crisis" in the life of the group.

Even if the group has completed its task(s), and there is no longer any clear reason for its continued existence, members will often find it difficult to let go of what may have proven to be an extremely fulfilling experience. Strong social bonds may have developed among group members, and people may feel attached to the group for the personal learning experience which it has provided. There are many needs in addition to accomplishing a task which can be met in a group. It is for these reasons that members may want to continue meeting beyond the natural life cycle of the group.

It is important for group members in this phase to acknowledge their apprehensions about ending the group, and to allow themselves to grieve its demise, and their separation from each other.

Some group leaders choose to help groups end by using ritual activities such as having every member give the others a symbolic "gift". Other facilitators may suggest an ending "celebration" such as a party or barbecue, perhaps including spouses or friends of group members.

Discussion about an "ending" experience may need to be initiated by the facilitator, especially if members are reluctant to disband the group. However, deciding on the actual format can be the group's final planning responsibility.

What if it's not the group which is ending — but your involvement with it?

It is possible that the group will choose to continue to meet, but will have reached a point in its maturity where it no longer needs a formal "facilitator".

The positive side of this picture is that you are now freed up to begin the process of developing another new group somewhere else. However, you also may need to acknowledge your attachment to the present group.

To continue the analogy, it's much like allowing your eldest child to move out on his/her own. You know that it's best for the child, but where does it leave you?

Expressing some of your feelings to the group may make it easier for you to say "good-bye", and will end your relationship with group members in a manner true to the norm of authenticity which you established from the start. Try not to deny those feelings. Voluntarily ending with a group which you have helped to "grow up" may be the biggest facilitation challenge of them all! ❖

A FINAL REFLECTION : Think back to your "vision" of the ideal group which you created at the start of this section.

What is preventing your group(s) from making this vision a reality?

_____

_____

_____

What could you, as the facilitator, do differently to help this happen? Set some realistically attainable goals for yourself as you think about your future work with groups.

_____

_____

_____

_____